Talking with Your Patients in English

Mitsuko Hirano
Christine D. Kuramoto
Ryota Ochiai

StreamLine

Web動画・音声ファイルのストリーミング再生について

CDマーク及びWeb動画マークがある箇所は、PC、スマートフォン、タブレット端末において、無料でストリーミング再生することができます。下記URLよりご利用ください。再生手順や動作環境などは本書巻末の「Web動画のご案内」をご覧ください。

http://st.seibido.co.jp

音声ファイルのダウンロードについて

CDマークがある箇所は、ダウンロードすることも可能です。下記URLより書籍を検索し、書籍詳細ページにあるダウンロードアイコンをクリックしてください。

https://www.seibido.co.jp

Talking with Your Patients in English

Copyright © 2019 by Mitsuko Hirano, Christine D. Kuramoto, Ryota Ochiai

All rights reserved for Japan.
No part of this book may be reproduced in any form
without permission from Seibido Co., Ltd.

はじめに

　外国人観光客をはじめ、日本で仕事をする外国人が増加し、病気やけがで病院を訪れ、入院される外国人が増えています。外国人の患者さんとのコミュニケーションを円滑にするための工夫が益々重要になっています。患者さんに最も身近に寄り添う看護師の臨床英語コミュニケーション能力向上は急務と言えます。さらに、臨床看護英語を少しでも活用することで、専門職者としてきちんと患者さんの情報を収集し、異なる文化や価値観を持つ人とも、考えや気持ちを伝えあおうとする姿勢を養う必要があります。

　本書は、将来臨床の現場で活躍する看護学生のために作られた、医療語彙・表現を中心とした初歩的な看護英語教材です。患者さんへのルーティン業務である巡回、状態観察、身の回りのお世話などの日々の業務が、患者さんに関する多くの情報をもたらします。そういった日常業務を通して、外国人の患者さんと英語でやりとりができれば、患者さんの回復に大いに貢献するでしょうし、患者さんにとっても大変心強いことでしょう。つたない英語を使ってでも、外国人の患者さんに寄り添おうとする看護師を患者さんはきっと信頼してくれます。

　本書は、看護の基本に忠実に、無理なく初歩的な看護英語を学べるような構成になっています。さらに、大きな特徴は、看護場面をアニメーションを使って再現していることです。アニメーションによって馴染みやすく、柔らかい看護場面を提供しています。患者さんとの基本的な英語でのやりとりが覚えられるようになっています。本書の特徴をまとめると以下の通りとなります。

　　a. 章の構成は、看護の学びに即した配置となっており、看護１年目の学生から使うことができます。
　　b. 患者さんとの会話練習では、アニメーションが使われ、臨床に即した会話を学ぶことができます。
　　c. 各章では、大きな Topic が２つずつ取り上げられており、事前学習を前提に、問題を解きながら学んでいくことができます。
　　d. 各章には、Medical Vocabulary が設けられ、関連した臨床医学医療語彙を学ぶことができます。

　本書を使って初歩的な臨床看護英語を学んだ看護学生が、将来、外国人の患者さんとの英語によるやりとりにさらに興味を持ち、また、自信を持って患者さんに寄り添い、ケアができるようになれば、著者としてこれ以上の喜びはありません。

　本書の刊行にあたっては、成美堂の佐野英一郎社長、編集の工藤隆志氏、アニメーションを制作してくださったフシギナの皆さんをはじめ多くの方々に多大なご尽力をいただきました。心から感謝申し上げます。

著者一同

本書の構成と使い方

✴ Expressions to Remember

　各章の warming-up として、使用頻度の高い重要な臨床看護表現を選択肢の問題として取り上げています。CD のリスニングでも聞き取れるようになっていますから、声を出して読み、しっかり覚えてください。

⊘ First Watching of the Animation

　外国人の患者さんと看護師とのやりとりを再現したアニメーション（約2分間）を視聴し、Yes、No などの問題に答える活動です。一度の視聴では、なかなか5問全てに解答するのは難しいかもしれません。何度も視聴し、事前学習として挑戦してください。

✎ Scenario: Second Watching & Dictation

　外国人の患者さんと看護師とのやりとりを視聴しながら、空所を埋めていく活動です。空所は看護師の発話が中心です。何度もやりとりを聴き、発話の趣旨を理解しながら埋めていきましょう。できるだけ事前学習をしておき、クラスで答えを確認する方法がお勧めです。出来上がった Scenario の看護師の部分は、極力暗記するようにしましょう。この Scenario を使って、シュミレーション演習をすることもできます。

✖ Comprehension Questions

　Scenario の内容理解を確認するための選択肢付きの設問です。できるだけ平易な設問が用意されていますが、Scenario がしっかり理解できたかが鍵になります。再度の視聴が必要になるかもしれません。

Focus Topics (Topic 1 & 2)

　各章で取り上げられている看護場面に関する、医療語彙・表現を学ぶ活動です。選択肢問題、穴埋め問題が多く併設されています。ただ表現を覚えるだけでなく、活動が与えられていることで、記憶に残りやすくなっています。また、この活動を通して、看護の学習にも触れられるようになっています。

▲ Medical Vocabulary

　Focus Topics で取り上げることができなかった医学医療語彙などをまとめています。臨床でよく使われる語彙が中心です。設問も用意されていて、正しい内容理解が促されるようになっています。発音に注意して、覚えるようにしましょう。

Chapter 7 と Chapter 14

　Chapter 7 と Chapter 14 では選択肢問題、穴埋め問題、クロスワードパズルなどの作業を通して、それまでの章のまとめができるようになっています。さらに、Chapter 7 の後半には、Medical Terminology に関する説明と設問があり、Chapter 14 の後半には、医療統計に関する英文読解が出来るようになっています。いずれも語彙を増やす活動の一環です。

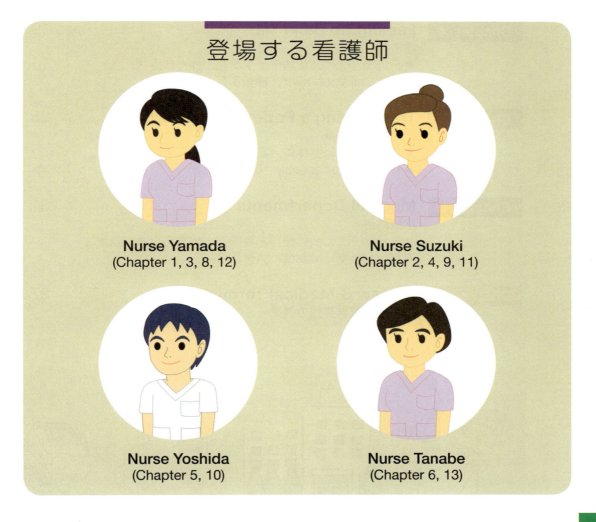

CONTENTS

はじめに ……………………………………………………………………… iii
本書の構成と使い方 ………………………………………………………… iv

Chapter 1 **Welcoming a Patient** …………………………………… 1
患者を迎える
- Focus Topics: 位置を示す表現／病院内施設
- Medical Vocabulary: 病室内備品

Chapter 2 **Taking Vital Signs** ……………………………………… 7
バイタルサイン測定
- Focus Topics: バイタルを測る機器類／看護物品
- Medical Vocabulary: 脈拍測定部位

Chapter 3 **Pain Assessment** ………………………………………… 13
痛みのアセスメント
- Focus Topics: 痛みを表す表現／痛みの問診術
- Medical Vocabulary: 体の部位名

Chapter 4 **Feeling So Sick!** ………………………………………… 19
症　状
- Focus Topics: 症状チェック表／様々な症状
- Medical Vocabulary: 検査項目

Chapter 5 **Transferring a Patient** ………………………………… 25
体位変換／移乗
- Focus Topics: 体位／動きの表現
- Medical Vocabulary: 歩行補助機器

Chapter 6 **Medical Departments** …………………………………… 31
診療科目
- Focus Topics: 診療科と専門医／検査のための表現
- Medical Vocabulary: 人体器官系

Chapter 7 **Review & Medical Terminology** ……………………… 37
まとめと医学英語の構造

Chapter 8 **Personal Care** 43
日常生活援助
- Focus Topics: 身だしなみ用具／日常生活援助表現
- Medical Vocabulary: 専門家との連携

Chapter 9 **Giving Medication to a Patient** 49
与　薬
- Focus Topics: 薬剤の種類／投薬指示関連の表現
- Medical Vocabulary: 薬の効能

Chapter 10 **Elimination (Bowel movement / Urination)** 55
排泄（排便／排尿）
- Focus Topics: 排泄の表現／排尿の仕組み
- Medical Vocabulary: 排便、排尿にかかわる語彙

Chapter 11 **Chronic Diseases** 61
慢性疾患
- Focus Topics: 患者情報収集／慢性病とは？
- Medical Vocabulary: 慢性疾患

Chapter 12 **Critical Care / Operating Room** 67
急性期／手術室
- Focus Topics: 救急室で／周手術期看護
- Medical Vocabulary: 集中治療室用語

Chapter 13 **Pregnancy Check-up** 73
妊婦健診
- Focus Topics: 妊娠初期・中期／陣痛と出産
- Medical Vocabulary: 産科用語

Chapter 14 **Review & Medical Reading** 79
まとめと医学英文読解

References 85

Chapter 1

患者を迎える

Welcoming a Patient

病院という慣れない環境に入院される患者さんには、わからないことや不安がたくさんあります。まずは笑顔で自己紹介をしてから、患者さんが入院中に困らないよう、病棟のつくりや今後の予定などを伝えていきましょう。

Expressions to Remember

Match the following Japanese expressions with the English ones below.

1. 本日の受け持ち看護師です。　　_____
2. 確認のためお名前をお伺いします。　_____
3. 車椅子に座ってください。　　　_____
4. この病衣に着替えてください。　_____
5. このナースコールを押してください。_____
6. 廊下を右にまっすぐ行った所です。_____
7. カーテンを閉めますね。　　　　_____
8. 10分で戻ってきます。　　　　　_____

- Please change into this hospital gown.
- I'm your attending nurse today.
- Push this nurse call button.
- May I have your name to confirm?
- I'll come back in 10 minutes.
- It's across the hall to the right.
- Please sit in this wheelchair.
- I'll close this curtain for you.

First Watching of the Animation

▶ Watch the animation and answer the following questions.

1. Did the nurse ask Ms. Tayler her birthday?　　　　　　　Yes.　No.
2. Is Ms. Tayler's room on the seventh floor?　　　　　　　Yes.　No.
3. Is her room a single?　　　　　　　　　　　　　　　　　Yes.　No.
4. Can Ms. Tayler use the cabinet for her clothes?　　　　Yes.　No.
5. Will the nurse close the curtain?　　　　　　　　　　　Yes.　No.

Chapter 1 Scenario: Second Watching & Dictation

◀ Watch the animation again and fill in the blanks.

Nurse: Ms. Tayler, I'm Nurse Yamada, ¹(   ) today.
Patient: Oh, hi.
Nurse: ²(   ) to confirm?
Patient: Jane Tayler.
Nurse: And your birthday?
Patient: May 11, 1965.
Nurse: Thank you, I'll take you to your room now. Please ³(   ).
Patient: Oh, I can walk.
Nurse: I know you can. But this is one of our regulations. Your room is in Ward 7 on the fifth floor. Ms. Tayler, ⁴(   ). Room 702.
Patient: It's not a single room, is it?
Nurse: No, you have three other ⁵(   ). Ms. Tayler, please ⁶(   ). Do you need any help?
Patient: No, I can do it myself.
Nurse: Ms. Tayler, this is ⁷(   ). Whenever you need someone, ⁸(   ).
Patient: Where can I put my clothes and personal items?
Nurse: Use this cabinet and the locker over there.
Patient: OK, and where is the bathroom? I need to go there first.
Nurse: ⁹(   ) to the right. Can you go there alone?
Patient: Oh, yes. No problem.
Nurse: Do you have any other questions?
Patient: No, not right now.
Nurse: ¹⁰(   ) for you now. I'll come back in 10 minutes.

◀ Watch the animation again and practice with your partner.

Chapter 1 Welcoming a Patient

⏩ Comprehension Questions

Answer the following questions.

1. What is Nurse Yamada going to do?
   (A) She is going to help Ms. Tayler go to the restroom.
   (B) She is going to take Ms. Tayler to her room.
   (C) She is going to help Ms. Tayler change into the hospital gown.
   (D) She is going to open the curtain.

2. Why does the nurse ask Ms. Tayler to sit in a wheelchair?
   (A) She cannot walk well.
   (B) She is very weak.
   (C) The nurse is following the hospital rule.
   (D) She doesn't have shoes.

3. Where can Ms. Tayler put her personal items?
   (A) She can use the cabinet and locker.
   (B) She can use the drawer.
   (C) She cannot keep her personal items anywhere.
   (D) She can put them behind the curtain.

4. Where is the bathroom?
   (A) It's behind the nurses' station.
   (B) It's next to the payphone on the right.
   (C) It's across from the patients' lounge.
   (D) It's across the hall to the right.

5. When will Nurse Yamada come back to Ms. Tayler?
   (A) in a few minutes   (B) in 10 minutes
   (C) in an hour   (D) She didn't say.

6. Fill in the blanks with the given words.

ask	spell out	give	call	fill in

   (1) Can you [   ] me your full name, please?
   (2) May I [   ] your name?
   (3) Can you [   ] your name?
   (4) Could you [   ] this form?
   (5) What would you like us to [   ] you?

▶ Watch the animation again and try to play the nurse's role.

3

FOCUS TOPICS

Topic 1 **Giving Directions** 位置を示す表現

病院内の様々な施設へ患者さんを案内するときに使う表現を学びましょう。前置詞を正しく使い分けましょう。 4

The restroom is **next to** the cashier.
The restroom is **on** your right.

A pay phone is **between** the cashier and pharmacy.

The nurses' station is **in front of** the elevator.
The nurses' station is **across from** the elevator.

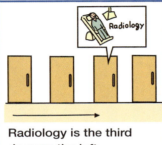

Radiology is the third door **on** the left.

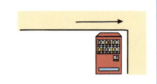

A vending machine is **in** the right corner.
It is on the right **down** the corridor.

The laboratory is **at the end of** the hall.
The laboratory is **down** the hall.

Q Choose the correct words in italics.

1. The nurses' station is *on / in* the left *under / down* the corridor.
2. The bathroom is *near / next* to the elevator.
3. Pay phones are *on / in* the first floor.
4. The restroom is *behind / across* from the nurses' station.
5. The conference room is *down / in front of* the hall.
6. The patients' cashier is *at / in* the end of the hall.
7. Walk past the pay phone and the ice machine is *at / in* the corner.

Chapter 1　Welcoming a Patient

Topic 2　Facilities in a Hospital　病院内施設

病院内には、外来受付、会計、医療福祉相談室など様々な施設があります。それぞれどんな役割があるか学びましょう。

Q Find the facilities below to match these definitions.

Definitions	Facilities
1. a place to pay your hospital bills	[　　]
2. a place to receive medical care such as injections and IV fluids	[　　]
3. a place where you can buy lunch or daily necessities	[　　]
4. a place to leave your urine or blood samples for examinations	[　　]
5. a place to get your medicines	[　　]
6. a place you visit when you are hospitalized	[　　]
7. for dietary education and counseling for patients	[　　]
8. a counter to register your name on your first visit	[　　]
9. for timely psychosocial intervention to patients and their families	[　　]
10. a place to get an X-ray taken	[　　]

 5

A radiology

B treatment room

C laboratory

D cashier

E pharmacy

F outpatient reception

G nutrition services

H hospital shop

I medical social services

J admission office

Medical Vocabulary Patient's Room 病室内備品

患者さんのごく身の回り、病室内にあるものは英語で何というのでしょうか。

Q1 Label the numbers using the words (A – J).

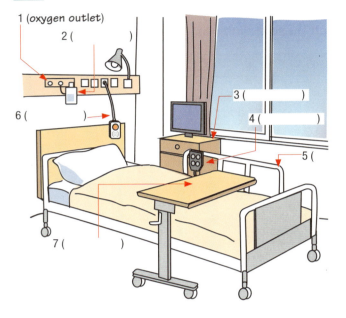
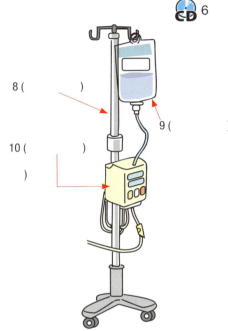

Q2 Match the Japanese words with the English ones.

(ア) ベッド柵
(イ) 床頭台
(ウ) ナースコールボタン
(エ) リモコン
(オ) オーバーベッドテーブル
(カ) 酸素プラグ
(キ) 吸引プラグ
(ク) 点滴台
(ケ) 輸液ポンプ
(コ) IV バッグ

(A) bedside cabinet
(B) suction outlet
(C) remote control
(D) side rail
(E) IV stand
(F) IV bag
(G) nurse call button
(H) overbed table
(I) infusion pump
(J) oxygen outlet

One Point 看護情報

英語で話しかけることが何より大切

慣れない英語で患者さんとコミュニケーションを取ろうとすると、どうしても「何をどう伝えればよいか」に目が行きがちです。しかし、あなたが英語を全く話せずに英語圏で入院することになった時、どんな気持ちになるかをまず考えてみてください。とても不安で心細いはずです。そんな時、片言でも日本語が話せる看護師さんがそばにいて、困っていることはないか聞いてくれたら、どれだけ心強いことでしょう。まず、英語で話しかけることが大切です。

Taking Vital Signs

バイタルサイン測定

バイタルサイン測定は看護の基本です。しかし、「マンシェットを腕に巻く」などの動作を伴うため、英語で行おうとすると意外に難しいものです。大切なことは、これから自分が何を行おうとしているか、患者さんに何をしてほしいかを、はっきりと伝えることです。結果を患者さんにフィードバックする表現も覚えておきましょう。

Expressions to Remember

 7

Match the following Japanese expressions with the English ones below.

1. 血圧を測ってみましょう。
2. マンシェットを巻きますね。
3. マンシェットが膨らみます。
4. 血圧は、140の95です。
5. 脈拍数は1分間に85回です。
6. 脇の下に体温計を入れてください。
7. 肺の音を聞かせてください。
8. 袖を捲ってください。

- I'll wrap this cuff around your arm.
- Let me listen to your breathing.
- Your pulse rate is 85 beats per minute.
- Let me take your blood pressure.
- I'll inflate the cuff.
- Put this thermometer under your arm.
- Please roll up your sleeve.
- Your blood pressure is 140 over 95.

First Watching of the Animation

   8

▶ Watch the animation and answer the following questions.

1. Did her nausea start this morning? Yes. No.
2. Did the nurse take her temperature? Yes. No.
3. Did the nurse take her pulse rate? Yes. No.
4. Does the patient have any other symptoms besides nausea? Yes. No.
5. Does the patient want to have an antiemetic injection? Yes. No.

Chapter 2 Scenario: Second Watching & Dictation

◀ Watch the animation again and fill in the blanks.

> *Buzz, buzz!*
> **Nurse:** Mrs. Chan, ¹(   )?
> **Patient:** Oh, nurse, I feel like I'm going to throw up.
> **Nurse:** Oh, OK. ²(   ) for you.
> Here it is. You can throw up if you have to.
> **Patient:** Thank you.
> **Nurse:** When did the nausea start?
> **Patient:** This morning.
> **Nurse:** Have you vomited since then?
> **Patient:** No, just a feeling like I might throw up.
> **Nurse:** ³(   ) now. I'll wrap this cuff around your arm.
> **Patient:** OK.
> **Nurse:** ⁴(   ). It's 140 over 95. It's a little bit higher than normal. ⁵(   ) now.
> **Patient:** How is it?
> **Nurse:** ⁶(   ). It's a bit fast but in normal range. Do you have any other symptoms, like a headache or numbness?
> **Patient:** Well, I feel very sluggish.
> **Nurse:** Your new medicines may have caused nausea and fatigue. Your doctor has prescribed an antiemetic. We can ⁷(   ) now.
> **Patient:** Antiemetic? What's that?
> **Nurse:** ⁸(   ) nausea and vomiting.
> **Patient:** OK. I need it.
> **Nurse:** I'll report this to your primary nurse. She'll give you a shot of that medicine right away.

◀ Watch the animation again and practice with your partner.

Chapter 2 Taking Vital Signs

⧓ Comprehension Questions

Answer the following questions.

1. What's the patient's problem?
   (A) The patient has a fever.
   (B) The patient feels sick.
   (C) The patient vomited.
   (D) The patient has a headache.

2. What is the nurse going to get for the patient?
   (A) a thermometer
   (B) medicine
   (C) a basin
   (D) a stethoscope

3. What was the patient's blood pressure?
   (A) 140/85   **(B)** 140/95
   (C) 130/85   **(D)** 135/95

4. What other symptoms does the patient have?
   (A) The patient lacks energy.
   (B) The patient has a headache.
   (C) The patient feels numbness in her leg.
   (D) The patient has a stomachache.

5. Read the following patient's data and fill in the blanks.

Patient name: Mrs. Mary Chan				Date: 09/25/2018	
BP	P	RR	T	CC	Nurse:
140/95	85	23	37.2	nausea	T. Suzuki

   (1) Mrs. Chan's blood pressure today is 140 (   ) 95.
   (2) Her pulse rate is 85 beats (   ) minute.
   (3) Her respiration rate is (   ) breaths per minute.
   (4) Her (   ) is thirty-seven (   ) two.
   (5) (   ) is her chief complaint (CC).

■◀ **Watch the animation again and try to play the nurse's role.**

9

FOCUS TOPICS

Topic 1 **Equipment to Take Vital Signs** バイタルを測る機器類

Vital signs（バイタルサイン）とは、患者さんの生命に関する最も基本的な情報のことで、「脈拍」「呼吸」「体温」「血圧」「意識レベル」などが基本です。客観的なデータをもとにアセスメントすることで、患者さんの全身状態の変化や異常の徴候を早めに発見できます。

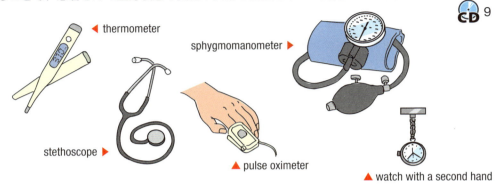

◀ thermometer
sphygmomanometer ▶
stethoscope ▶
▲ pulse oximeter
▲ watch with a second hand

CD 9

Q1 Fill in the names of equipment in the blanks.

1. A (   ) is used to measure a patient's blood pressure.
2. A (   ) is used to measure a patient's body temperature.
3. A (   ) is used to listen to heart sounds.
4. A (   ) is used to measure the concentration of oxygen in the blood.
5. A (   ) is needed to measure a patient's pulse and respiration rate per minute.

Q2 Fill in the blanks or choose the best answer.

1. What are main vital signs? (   ) (   )
   (   ) (   )
2. What are these temperatures called?
   A temperature taken in the mouth is a/an (*rectal / oral / axillary*) temperature.
   A temperature taken under the arm is a/an (*rectal / oral / axillary*) temperature.
   A temperature taken in the rectum is a/an (*rectal / oral / axillary*) temperature.
3. What do you need to take a patient's blood pressure?
   (   ), (   )
4. What is **systolic pressure**? It is the *higher / lower* number of the blood pressure.
5. What is **diastolic pressure**? It is the *higher / lower* number of the blood pressure.

Chapter 2　Taking Vital Signs

Topic 2　Nursing Equipment　看護物品

看護師が使う物品には、様々なものがあります。ワゴンは日本語です。英語では cart と言います。絆創膏、ピンセットを英語で正しく言えますか。

Q Fill in the blanks with the items below.

1. A/An (　　　　　) is for soiled dressings and other medical waste.
2. A/An (　　　　　) is a device for compression of an artery or vein.
3. A/An (　　　　　) is used to check light reflexes of your patient.
4. A/An (　　　　　) is a complete record of a patient's clinical data and medical history.
5. A/An (　　　　　) is used as a cold compress to alleviate pain or swelling.
6. A/An (　　　　　) is used to cover a wound and keep it clean.
7. A/An (　　　　　) is used to transport nursing items.
8. (　　　　　) are used for picking up small objects.
9. A/An (　　　　　) is a tool used for examination of the mouth and throat.
10. A/An (　　　　　) is used to inject fluid into, or withdraw fluid from, the body.

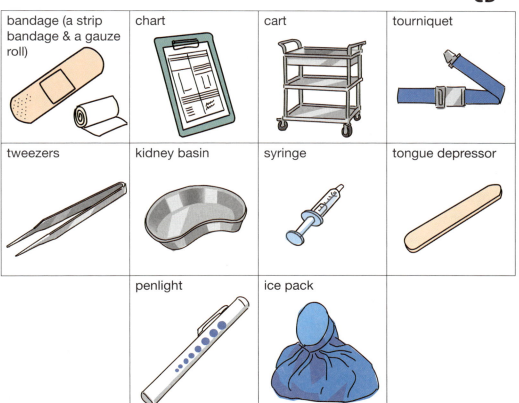

bandage (a strip bandage & a gauze roll)	chart	cart	tourniquet
tweezers	kidney basin	syringe	tongue depressor
	penlight	ice pack	

Medical Vocabulary　Arterial Pulse Points　脈拍測定部位

脈拍は、一般に手関節の母指に近い部分を走行している橈骨動脈で測定されます。それは、橈骨動脈が皮膚に近い部分を走行し、体表から拍動に触れやすいからです。他の部位でも、脈拍を触知あるいは計測することができます。どんな部位でしょうか。

Q1 Label the numbers using the words (A – H).

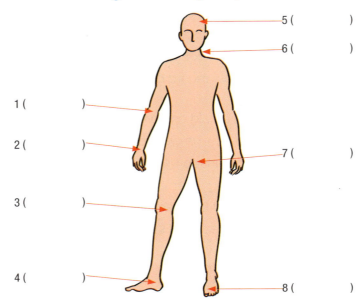

1 (　　　)
2 (　　　)
3 (　　　)
4 (　　　)
5 (　　　)
6 (　　　)
7 (　　　)
8 (　　　)

Q2 Match the artery in English with the ones in Japanese.

(A) temporal artery
(B) carotid artery
(C) brachial artery
(D) radial artery
(E) femoral artery
(F) popliteal artery
(G) posterior tibial artery
(H) dorsalis pedis artery

(ア) 橈骨動脈（とうこつ）
(イ) 頸動脈（けい）
(ウ) 後脛骨動脈（こうけいこつ）
(エ) 側頭動脈（そくとう）
(オ) 膝窩動脈（しっか）
(カ) 足背動脈（そくはい）
(キ) 上腕動脈（じょうわん）
(ク) 大腿動脈（だいたい）

One Point 看護情報

単位が問題だ

いざバイタルサイン測定の結果を患者さんにフィードバックしようとして、英語表現に自信がないことに気づくのが、単位に関する表現です。例えば、血圧の「120/60mmHg」は、英語では、one hundred twenty over sixty millimeter of mercury となりますが、表現がぱっと思いつかないのではないでしょうか。さらに、体温の測定では日本では「摂氏 Celsius」ですが、アメリカをはじめとする一部英語圏では「華氏 Fahrenheit」が用いられます。そんな国からきている患者さんは、摂氏で言われてもピンと来ないかもしれません。換算表などを用意して対応したいですね。

Chapter 3

Pain Assessment

痛みのアセスメント

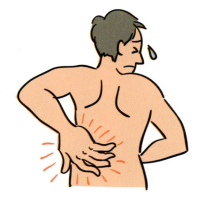

痛みは主観的な体験です。患者さんが自分の体験を表現できるよう、痛みの日常生活への影響、パターン、強さ、部位、性状などを尋ねていきましょう。体の各部位の名称や、痛みの種類を表す表現を覚えておくと、適切なアセスメントに役立ちます。

✦ Expressions to Remember 12

Match these Japanese expressions with the English ones below.

1. どこが痛いですか。 _____
2. いつ痛み出しましたか。 _____
3. どのくらいの期間、痛みがありましたか。 _____
4. どんな痛みか言えますか。 _____
5. 0から10では、どのくらいの痛みですか。 _____
6. 痛みは広がっていますか。 _____
7. 痛みの他に別の症状はありますか。 _____
8. 今痛み止めが必要ですか。 _____

- Does the pain radiate/move anywhere?
- Can you describe your pain?
- Do you have any other symptoms besides pain?
- When did your pain start?
- How long did the pain last?
- Do you want a painkiller now?
- On a scale of 0 to 10, how would you rate your pain?
- Where exactly is the pain?

◯ First Watching of the Animation   13

▶ Watch the animation and answer the following questions.

1. Did Mr. Miller sleep well last night? Yes. No.
2. Does Mr. Miller need a painkiller? Yes. No.
3. Did the pain start in the morning? Yes. No.
4. Was the pain score higher than five? Yes. No.
5. Was his blood pressure 120 over 85? Yes. No.

Chapter 3 Scenario: Second Watching & Dictation

◀ Watch the animation again and fill in the blanks.

Nurse: Good morning, Mr. Miller. Did you sleep well last night?
Patient: Good morning, Nurse Yamada. Well, no, I didn't.
Nurse: No? Why was that?
Patient: I had pain in my lower back.
Nurse: Oh, I'm sorry to hear that. ¹(　　　　　　　　　　　)?
Patient: It started in the middle of the night.
Nurse: ²(　　　　　　　　　　　)?
Patient: Right here, near my bottom.
Nurse: ³(　　　　　　　　　　　) your pain?
Patient: I don't know how to do that.
Nurse: Oh, is the pain sharp, burning, or squeezing?
Patient: Um… It is a squeezing pain.
Nurse: ⁴(　　　　　　　　　　　) have the pain?
Patient: Yes, it still hurts.
Nurse: ⁵(　　　　　　　　　　　) 0 to 10, how would you rate your pain? Zero is no pain and 10 is the worst pain you ever had.
Patient: Oh, well, six or seven.
Nurse: It must be really painful, then. ⁶(　　　　　　　　　　　) now?
Patient: Yes, please.
Nurse: OK, I'll bring it soon.
Let me take your blood pressure first. Is that OK with you?
Patient: Yes, that's fine.
Nurse: I'll ⁷(　　　　　　　　　　　) your upper arm.
Patient: OK.
Nurse: Do you have any other symptoms besides the pain in your back?
Patient: No, nothing else.
Nurse: It's done.
Patient: How is it?
Nurse: 130 over 95. It's not bad. I'll come back ⁸(　　　　　　　　　　　) right away.

◀ Watch the animation again and practice with your partner.

14

Chapter 3 Pain Assessment

⋈ Comprehension Questions

Answer the following questions.

1. What was Mr. Miller's trouble?
  (A) He had a headache.
  (B) He had a toothache.
  (C) He had a backache.
  (D) He had a stomachache.

2. When did the pain start?
  (A) It started in the middle of the night.
  (B) It started after dinner.
  (C) It just started.
  (D) It started in the morning.

3. On a scale of 0 to 10, how did he rate his pain?
  (A) 4 or 5
  (B) 2 or 3
  (C) 6 or 7
  (D) 8 or 10

4. How did he describe his pain?
  (A) sharp
  (B) throbbing
  (C) burning
  (D) squeezing

5. Which of the following is true?
  (A) The nurse gave the painkiller to the patient.
  (B) The nurse took his blood pressure before she gave him a painkiller.
  (C) The patient has other symptoms besides pain in the back.
  (D) The patient has pain in his upper back.

◼◀ Watch the animation again and try to play the nurse's role.

15

FOCUS TOPICS

Topic 1 **Expressing Pains** 痛みを表す表現

英語では「～が痛いです」を表す表現が、何通りかあります。

I have (a) pain in my ～.　My ～ aches.　My ～ hurts.

お腹が痛い。　　　• I have (a) pain in my stomach.
　　　　　　　　　• My stomach aches.
　　　　　　　　　• My stomach hurts.
　　　　　　　　　• I have a stomachache.

Ache / Pain / Hurt の違い

Ache: 一般的には特定の場所に起こる不快感を表します。pain よりも長引く痛みを指します。a headache, a stomachache, a backache, a toothache, an earache の 5 つの複合語があります。ache は、動詞としても使われます。
　例）My back really aches. My back is really aching.

Pain: ache に比べて pain は「もっと強くて無視できない痛み」を指します。
　例）I suddenly felt a lot of pain in my stomach yesterday.

Hurt: 痛みとしては ache と pain の両方の痛みを表します。具体的な部位を主語にして使われることが多いです。たとえば、My shoulder hurts. のように。また、hurt は、外傷を表す時にも使われます。
　例）I hurt my finger badly yesterday.

Sore: 形容詞として使われます。「傷や炎症によるひりひりした痛み」を指します。
　例）I have a sore throat.　My throat is sore.

Q **Complete the sentences using the given words. You may need certain changes in words.**

ache	pain	sore	hurt

1. I felt a sharp _____ in my back.

2. Three people were _____ in the accident.

3. I have a terrible _____ throat.

4. I can't sleep because my head _____ too bad.

5. Oh, my back! It is _____ing.

6. I have a terrible stomach _____.

7. She says her stomach is still _____ after the operation.

Chapter 3　Pain Assessment

Topic 2　PQRST　痛みの問診術

しっかり押さえておくべき内容を忘れないようにするためにアメリカの医学生や看護学生はよく acronym（頭字語）を用いた mnemonic（ニモーニック・記憶法）を使います。痛みの問診では、「PQRST が大切だ」と覚えます。

 14

1)　P: Provocation/Palliation ＝「誘因または緩和」どんな時に良くなるか、または悪くなるのか。
　　• What makes your pain better?　　• What makes your pain worse?
　　• What have you tried to relieve your pain?

2)　Q: Quality/Quantity ＝「質または量」どんな痛みか表現する。
　　• Can you describe your pain?
　　• What type of pain is it?

3)　R: Region/Radiation ＝「部位または放散」痛みの場所、痛みは広がっているか。
　　• Where is your pain?
　　• Does the pain move anywhere?

4)　S: Severity/Scale ＝「重症度スケールを活用した情報」どのくらい痛いか。
　　• On a scale of 0 to 10 with 0 being no pain and 10 being the worst pain you can imagine, how would you rate your pain?
　　• How bad is the pain?

5)　T: Timing ＝「時間に関する情報」いつから、どのくらいの頻度で、どのくらい続いているか。
　　• When did it start?
　　• How often does it occur?
　　• How long does it last?

Q　Fill in the blanks.

15

Patient: I've got terrible back pain.
　Nurse: Oh, I see. Can you tell me _____ exactly the pain is?
Patient: In my lower back. Here.
　Nurse: Does the pain _____ anywhere?
Patient: No. It stays where it is.
　Nurse: How would you _____ your pain on a _____ of 0 to 10.
Patient: Oh, well, it's an eight.
　Nurse: It must be very _____.

17

Medical Vocabulary　The Body Parts　体の部位名

患者さんのケアをする時に、英語では体の部位をどのように言うのかしっかり、身につけておきましょう。

Q Label the numbers using the words (A – T).　CD 16

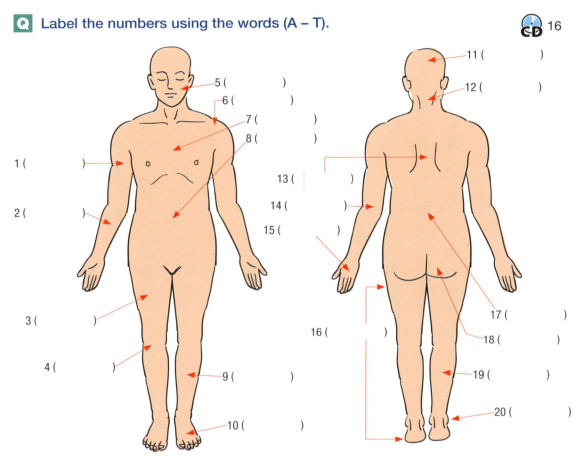

(A) stomach	(B) knee	(C) head	(D) back	(E) calf
(F) foot	(G) leg	(H) upper arm	(I) shin	(J) shoulder
(K) forearm	(L) face	(M) thigh	(N) hand	(O) lower back
(P) neck	(Q) bottom	(R) elbow	(S) chest	(T) ankle

One Point 看護情報

英語で共感的態度を示そう

PQRST に沿って痛みの問診を進め、患者さんの重症度や緊急度を判断することは、看護師の重要な役割ですが、痛みを訴える患者さんに共感的態度で接することも大切です。最も使いやすい表現は、"Are you OK?" だと思います。ほかにも、"I'm sorry (to hear that)." "That's too bad." "It must be so hard for you." などの表現も使うことができます。問診が一方的なものにならないよう、使いやすい表現を覚えておきましょう。

Chapter 4

症状

Feeling So Sick!

患者さんに必要なケアを行うためには、症状をアセスメントすることが大切です。まず、代表的な症状を表す英語表現を覚えましょう。次に、患者さんが自分の症状について正確、かつ主体的に話せるように、開かれた質問 Open Question と閉じられた質問 Closed Question を使い分けてみましょう。

✦ Expressions to Remember 17

Match the following Japanese expressions with the English ones below.

1. どんな症状がありますか。　　_____
2. これらの症状はいつ始まりましたか。　_____
3. 症状を抑えるために何かしましたか。　_____
4. 手のしびれのような症状はありますか。　_____
5. このようなことは、何回くらいありましたか。　_____
6. この症状はどれくらい続いていますか。　_____
7. 靴を脱いで計器に乗ってください。　_____
8. 肩を楽にして背筋を伸ばしてください。　_____

- How many times has this happened?
- How long have you had the symptom?
- Relax your shoulders and stand straight.
- Did you try to control the symptoms?
- What symptoms do you have?
- When did these symptoms start to appear?
- Could you take off your shoes and step on the scale?
- Do you have any symptoms like numbness in your hands?

◯ First Watching of the Animation   18

▶ Watch the animation and answer the following questions.

1. Did the nurse only measure the patient's height?　　Yes.　No.
2. Did the patient lose weight?　　Yes.　No.
3. Does the patient have painful urination?　　Yes.　No.
4. Does the patient feel tired?　　Yes.　No.
5. Does the patient have tingling in his feet?　　Yes.　No.

Chapter 4 Scenario: Second Watching & Dictation

◀ Watch the animation again and fill in the blanks.

Nurse: Hello, Mr. Smith. I'm Nurse Suzuki. I'd like to ask you a few questions before your doctor sees you. Is it OK with you?

Patient: Sure, go ahead.

Nurse: Thank you. First of all, I'd like to know your height and weight. Could you take off your shoes and ¹(   ) with your back against the pole?

Patient: OK. Like this?

Nurse: ²(   ) and stand straight. Yes, that's fine. Well, 65 kg and 178 cm tall.

Patient: I've lost three or four kilograms these days, even though I eat a lot.

Nurse: Is that so? Please ³(   ).

Patient: Thank you.

Nurse: Well, do you have ⁴(   ) that worry you besides weight loss?

Patient: Oh, well, I need to go to the bathroom a lot, especially at night. I ⁵(   ) so I drink a lot.

Nurse: ⁶(   ) to the bathroom at night?

Patient: Three or four times.

Nurse: What else?

Patient: I feel very tired.

Nurse: I see. When did these ⁷(   )?

Patient: Oh, well, I've had these problems for a month or so.

Nurse: Do you have any symptoms like numbness in your hands or ⁸(   )?

Patient: Oh, yes. I notice tingling in my feet sometimes. But I don't think I have vision problems.

Nurse: All right, Mr. Smith, Dr. Tanaka will see you in a minute.

◀ Watch the animation again and practice with your partner.

Chapter 4 Feeling So Sick!

▶◀ Comprehension Questions

Answer the following questions.

1. What did the nurse do before she asked the patient a few questions?
   (A) She took his temperature.
   (B) She only weighed him.
   (C) She measured his height and weight.
   (D) She took his blood pressure.

2. What other symptoms does the patient have besides weight loss?
   (A) frequent urination
   (B) loss of appetite
   (C) diarrhea
   (D) shortness of breath

3. When did these symptoms start to appear?
   (A) a few months ago
   (B) a year ago
   (C) a week ago
   (D) a month ago

4. How often does the patient go to the toilet at night?
   (A) one time
   (B) two times
   (C) three or four times
   (D) more than four times

5. What other symptoms does the nurse ask the patient about?
   (A) nausea
   (B) tingling
   (C) bleeding
   (D) edema

▨◀ Watch the animation again and try to play the nurse's role.

21

FOCUS TOPICS

Topic 1 **Symptoms Checker** 症状チェック表

初期の2型糖尿病（type 2 diabetes）は自覚症状（symptoms）がほとんどありません。自覚症状が出た時には、すでに合併症（complications）が進んでいることも少なくありませんから早めに症状を知る必要があります。以下の図は、代表的な糖尿病の症状を示しています。

Q1 Check if Mr. Smith in the dialogue has the following symptoms or not. 19

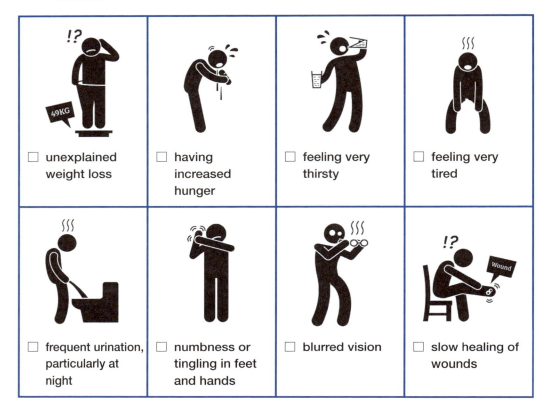

Q2 Put the words in the correct order. 20

1. Can you [me, symptoms, describe, the, to]?
2. When did [ill, start, you, feeling]?
3. How [is, pain, bad, the]?
4. What were you [the, appeared, when, doing, symptom]?
5. How [last, did, the, long, symptom]?
6. Do you [have, still, symptom, the]?
7. Have [symptoms, noticed, any, you, other]?
8. Have [this, had, you, of, symptom, kind] before?

Chapter 4　Feeling So Sick!

Topic 2　List of Symptoms　様々な症状

患者さんは、様々な症状（symptoms）を訴えて、病院を訪れます。その中でも、最も強い訴えを主訴（CC: Chief Complaint）といいます。体に起こる症状を知ることで、病気が早期に発見されます。患者さんが訴える症状にはどんなものがあるでしょうか。

 21

熱 fever / feverish	鼻水 runny nose	鼻づまり stuffy nose / blocked nose	咳 cough
悪寒 chill	おう吐 vomiting	吐き気 nausea	湿疹 / 発疹 rash
脱水 dehydration	息切れ shortness of breath	黄疸 jaundice	食欲不振 loss of appetite
胸やけ heartburn	かゆみ itch	出血 bleeding / hemorrhage	めまい dizziness / vertigo
不眠 sleeplessness / insomnia	けいれん seizure	ぜん鳴 wheezing	浮腫 swelling / edema

Q　Fill in the blanks using symptoms above.

1. I have a twisted ankle. It caused swelling. = The patient has (　　　　　).
2. I feel sick to my stomach. = The patient has (　　　　　).
3. My baby has a yellowish discoloration of the skin. = The baby has (　　　　　).
4. I cannot sleep at night. = The patient has (　　　　　).
5. My grandmother has been working in the garden under the blazing sun so long. She may have (　　　　　).
6. My father has difficulty breathing. = He has (　　　　　).

23

Medical Vocabulary — Medical Tests 検査項目

病気を特定するためには、患者さんが訴える自覚症状の他に、客観的に患者さんの状態を測定するための様々な検査が必要となります。どんな検査があるでしょうか。

体液検査　Analysis of Body Fluids	
血液検査	blood test, hemanalysis
尿検査	urine test, urinalysis
検便	stool analysis
喀痰検査	sputum culture
画像検査　Imaging Tests	
胸部X線検査	chest X-ray
コンピューター断層撮影	computed tomography (CT)
磁気共鳴断層撮影	magnetic resonance imaging (MRI)
血管造影	angiography
超音波検査	ultrasonography
内視鏡検査　Endoscopy	
気管支鏡検査	bronchoscopy
上部消化管内視鏡検査	esophagogastroduodenoscopy, EGD test
大腸内視鏡検査	colonoscopy
機能検査　Measurement of Body Functions	
心電図検査	electrocardiography (ECG/EKG)
筋電図検査	electromyography (EMG)
脳波検査	electroencephalography (EEG)
肺機能検査	pulmonary function test
肺活量検査	spirometry

Q Find the names of medical tests above and complete the sentences.

1. [　　　　　] measures how much air you can inhale and exhale.
2. To check the inner lining of your large intestine, [　　　　] is used.
3. A [　　　　] is a test to detect and identify bacteria or fungi that are infecting the lungs or breathing passages.
4. [　　　　　] uses ultrasound waves to produce images of internal organs and tissues.

One Point 看護情報

問診は重要だ！

少し古い話になりますが、1982年に発表された論文[1]において、内科医が患者さんの正確な診断名にたどり着く割合は、問診後が76%、その後の身体診察後が12%、さらにその後の検査後が11%だったと報告されています。患者さんが抱えている問題を適切に把握するために、問診がどれだけ大切かを示す報告だと思います。問診には語学力が欠かせません。語学力を高めることは、問診を通して患者さんに良い医療を提供することでもあります。

(1) は巻末の References を参照。

Chapter 5

Transferring a Patient

体位変換／移乗

体をうまく動かせない患者さんの体位を変換する、ベッドから車椅子、車椅子からベッドへ移すなど、体位変換や移乗は患者さんを守る大切な業務です。英語表現には特徴的な言い回しがあります。しっかり覚えて、患者さんに安心感を与えてください。

Expressions to Remember

 23

Match the following Japanese expressions with the English ones below.

1. 今から放射線科にお連れします。 _____
2. ベッドから出るお手伝いをしますね。 _____
3. ベッドの端にお座りになれますか。 _____
4. 横になっていただけますか。 _____
5. しばらく座ったままでいてください。 _____
6. どうぞ私にもたれてください。 _____
7. 足置きに足を乗せてください。 _____
8. 車椅子を押しますね。 _____

- Stay seated for a few moments.
- Please lie on your side.
- I'll push the wheelchair for you.
- Can you sit up on the edge of the bed?
- I'd like to take you to radiology now.
- I'll help you get out of the bed.
- You can lean on me.
- Place your feet on the footrests.

First Watching of the Animation

 24

▶ Watch the animation and answer the following questions.

1. Is the nurse going to take Ms. Wong to the laboratory?   Yes. No.
2. Could the patient sit up on the edge of the bed?   Yes. No.
3. Did the patient feel dizzy when she sat on the bed?   Yes. No.
4. Is the patient going to move the wheelchair by herself?   Yes. No.
5. Is Ms. Wong expecting her husband this morning?   Yes. No.

25

Chapter 5 Scenario: Second Watching & Dictation

   24

◀ Watch the animation and fill in the blanks.

Nurse: Hello, Ms. Wong. How are you feeling now?
Patient: Oh, Nurse Yoshida. I'm OK.
Nurse: Your doctor has ordered an X-ray. I'd like to ¹(   ) to radiology now if it's OK with you.
Patient: What X-ray is that?
Nurse: It's a chest X-ray.
Patient: OK.
Nurse: I'll help you get out of the bed. Can you ²(   ) of the bed?
Patient: Yes. Give me some time.
Nurse: Just ³(   ). First, please ⁴(   ). I'll bend your knees. Take my arms so I can help you. There! How are you feeling?
Patient: I feel light-headed.
Nurse: ⁵(   ) for a few moments.
Patient: Thank you. I'm fine now.
Nurse: Good. Let me help you put on your shoes. Then I'll help you to stand up. Take my arms. One, two, three. You can ⁶(   ).
Patient: OK.
Nurse: Place your hand on the armrest here and sit down slowly. OK?
Patient: Yes.
Nurse: Good. That's it. Then ⁷(   ) on the footrests. I'll ⁸(   ) for you.
Patient: I'm expecting my daughter this morning. Do you mind if I leave a note to tell her that I've gone for an X-ray?
Nurse: No problem.
Patient: Where is radiology?
Nurse: It's on the first basement floor, B1. We'll take the elevator. Are you ready to go now? Here we go.

◀ Watch the animation again and practice with your partner.

Chapter 5 Transferring a Patient

Comprehension Questions

Answer the following questions.

Q1 What is the patient or the nurse doing? Find answers in the animation.

1. The patient is sitting ( ) of the bed.	2. The nurse is ( ) the patient's knees.
3. The nurse is ( ) the patient roll onto her side.	4. The patient is ( ) the nurse.
5. The patient is ( ) on the footrests.	6. The nurse is ( ) the patient's wheelchair.

Q2 Fill in the blanks with the given words.

up	on	on	down	with	out	for

1. I'd like to take you to radiology if it's OK (   ) you.
2. I'll help you get (   ) of the bed.
3. Please lie (   ) your side.
4. Can you sit (   ) on the edge of the bed?
5. Please stay seated (   ) a few moments.
6. Let me help you put (   ) your shoes.
7. Please sit (   ) slowly.

▶ Watch the animation again and try to play the nurse's role.

27

FOCUS TOPICS

Topic 1　**Patient Positioning**　体位

自分自身で身動きが取れない患者さんに対し、看護師や介護者が定期的に体の向きを変えることを体位変換（patient positioning / position change）といいます。長時間同じ部分が圧迫され、不動の状態が続くと血行不良が起こり褥瘡（pressure sores / bed sores）や拘縮（contracture）の原因となります。体位変換によってそのような合併症（complication）を防ぎます。どのような体位があるでしょうか。

Q Fill in the blanks with the given words. 25

```
down    stomach    side    forward    supine    up    head    back
```

仰臥位：dorsal (supine) position
- The patient lies on her ¹(   ).
- She lies face ²(   ).

腹臥位：prone position
- The patient lies on her ³(   ).
- She lies face ⁴(   ).

側臥位：lateral (side-lying) position
- The patient lies on one side of her body.
- She lies on her ⁵(   ).

ファウラー位（半座位）：Fowler's position
A variation of the ⁶(   ) position, in which the head of the bed is elevated to between 45 and 60 degrees.

セミファウラー位：semi-Fowler's position
He lies with his ⁷(   ) raised 15 to 45 degrees.

起座位：orthopneic position
The patient sits up and bends ⁸(   ) to make breathing easier.

Chapter 5 | Transferring a Patient

Topic 2 Body Movements 動きの表現

患者さんの体位を変換し、ベッドから車椅子、車椅子からベッドへの移乗をサポートするためには、体の動きを英語でしっかり表現する必要があります。

Q1 Find expressions below to match the following illustrations. 26

(A) Bend your fingers.	(B) Twist your body to the right.
(C) Stretch your back.	(D) Rotate your head from left to right.
(E) Raise your arms in the air.	(F) Lift up your heels.
(G) Stand on tiptoe.	(H) Make a fist.

Q2 What position is this called?

| supine position | lateral position | prone position |
| Fowler's position | semi-Fowler's position | orthopneic position |

1. A patient is supine and the head of the bed is elevated to 45 to 60 degrees.	[ ]
2. A patient is lying on her side.	[ ]
3. A patient has difficulties in breathing and sits upright in a bed, possibly bending forward.	[ ]
4. A patient is lying on her stomach.	[ ]

29

Medical Vocabulary — Assistive Devices for Mobility　歩行補助機器

外国人の患者さんを安全に車椅子に移動するためには、車椅子の各部位を英語でしっかり言えることが大切です。

Q Label the numbers using the given words. 27

backrest　footrest　hand rim　brake　caster　grip　wheel　seat　leg rest　armrest

1 (　　　)　2 (　　　)　3 (　　　)　4 (　　　)　5 (　　　)　6 (　　　)　7 (　　　)　8 (　　　)　9 (　　　)　10 (　　　)

その他の歩行補助用具： 28

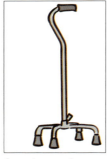
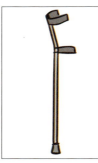

four-legged cane　　forearm crutch　　crutches　　walker　　foot orthosis

One Point 看護情報

ちょっとした注意喚起の表現

看護の仕事は「臨機応変」が大切です。看護師には、「何かおかしい」「危ないな」と思った時に、とっさの対応が求められます。移乗時に怖いのは転倒、転落です。ふとした時に注意を促すフレーズを覚えておきましょう。

- Watch your step! 足元に気をつけて。
- Heads up! 気をつけて。危ない。
- Please take it easy. 無理をしないで。頑張りすぎないで。
- Behind you! 背後に気をつけて。
- Take your time! ゆっくりね。

Chapter 6

診療科目

Medical Departments

患者さんを必要な診療科に案内するには、その診療科でどんな患者さんを診るのか知っていないとできません。また、各部門での代表的な検査で用いる英語表現や、人体の器官の英語名を覚えておく必要もありますね。

Expressions to Remember

 29

Match the following Japanese expressions with the English ones below.

1. どうされましたか。　　　　　　　　　_____
2. どの科に行けばいいでしょうか。　　　_____
3. 泌尿器科に行ってください。　　　　　_____
4. 内分泌科はホルモンの病気を扱います。_____
5. 手をひどく火傷しました。　　　　　　_____
6. 娘が甲状腺の病気だと診断されました。_____
7. 娘は内分泌科に紹介されました。　　　_____
8. お大事に。　　　　　　　　　　　　　_____

- Go to the urology department.
- My daughter has been referred to endocrinology.
- How can I help you?
- Take care.
- Which department should I go to?
- The endocrinology department deals with hormonal diseases.
- My daughter has been diagnosed with thyroid disease.
- I burned my hand really badly.

First Watching of the Animation

 30

▶ Watch the animation and answer the following questions.

1. Does the first outpatient have frequent urination?　　Yes.　No.
2. Does he have a fever?　　Yes.　No.
3. Did the second outpatient go to the treatment room?　　Yes.　No.
4. Does the girl have thyroid disease?　　Yes.　No.
5. Does the mother of the girl have a medical referral letter?　　Yes.　No.

31

Chapter 6 Scenario: Second Watching & Dictation

 30

■◀ Watch the animation and fill in the blanks.

At the general information desk:

Nurse: Hi, good morning. ¹(　　　　　　　　　　)?

Patient A: Yes, I need to go to the toilet often in the middle of the night. So I can't sleep very well. Which department should I go to?

Nurse: Do you have any other symptoms, like fever or stomachache?

Patient A: No, I don't.

Nurse: Well, then ²(　　　　　　　　　　). First visit the No. 8 reception desk.

Patient A: Thank you.

Nurse: You're welcome. Take care.

Patient B: Good morning. I ³(　　　　　　　　　　) really badly when I was using a gas burner. Can I go to the treatment room now?

Nurse: Oh, I'm sorry to hear that. But first our dermatologist will see you. And he will decide ⁴(　　　　　　　　　　).

Patient B: Derma…?

Nurse: Dermatologist. A skin doctor.

Patient B: Oh, I see.

Nurse: Go to the second floor of Building B. Visit the No.10 reception desk. Take the escalator over there.

Patient B: Thank you.

Nurse: May I help you, ma'am?

Patient C: Yes. My daughter has ⁵(　　　　　　　　　　) thyroid disease. And she ⁶(　　　　　　　　　　) this hospital. But we don't know which department we should go to.

Nurse: All right. May I see your ⁷(　　　　　　　　　　)?

Patient C: Here it is.

Nurse: Well, your daughter has been referred to our endocrinologist.

Patient C: Endo…?

Nurse: Endocrinologist. It is a specialist dealing with hormonal diseases. Go to the No. 5 reception desk. Go straight down the hall. You can find it in front of you. ⁸(　　　　　　　　　　).

■◀ Watch the animation again and practice with your partner.

Chapter 6 Medical Departments

▶◀ Comprehension Questions

Answer the following questions.

1. What's the problem of the first outpatient?
(A) He has difficulties urinating.
(B) He has hematuria.
(C) He has frequent urination at night.
(D) He has come to have a urine test.

2. What is dermatologist?
(A) a child physician
(B) a skin doctor
(C) a hormone doctor
(D) a bone doctor

3. What brings the second outpatient to the hospital?
(A) He burned his hand badly.
(B) He cut his finger.
(C) He has a stomachache.
(D) He wants to get an injection.

4. What has the girl been diagnosed with?
(A) heart disease
(B) skin disease
(C) mental disease
(D) hormonal disease

5. What is a medical referral letter?
(A) It's a letter to discharge a patient.
(B) It's a letter for a patient to get a specific medicine.
(C) It's a letter to send a patient to another physician for a specific problem.
(D) It's a letter for you to get a specific job in a hospital.

■◀ **Watch the animation again and try to play the nurse's role.**

33

FOCUS TOPICS

Topic 1 Medical Departments & Specialists 診療科と専門医

病院には様々な診療科があり、様々な専門医が診療に当たっています。どのような症状がある時に、それらの診療科を訪れるのでしょうか。 31

日本語	英語診療名	専門医
小児科	pediatrics	pediatrician
泌尿器科	urology	urologist
内分泌科	endocrinology	endocrinologist
整形外科	orthopedics	orthopedist
産科	obstetrics	obstetrician
婦人科	gynecology	gynecologist
産婦人科	obstetrics and gynecology = OBGYN	
外科	surgery	surgeon
腫瘍科	oncology	oncologist
胃腸科	gastroenterology	gastroenterologist
脳神経外科	neurosurgery	neurosurgeon
耳鼻咽喉科	otorhinolaryngology = ENT	otorhinolaryngologist
呼吸器科	pulmonology/respiratory medicine	pulmonologist
皮膚科	dermatology	dermatologist
腎臓病科	nephrology	nephrologist
精神科	psychiatry	psychiatrist
循環器科	cardiovascular medicine	cardiologist
内科	internal medicine	internist

Q Which medical department should I go to? Find departments from the list above.

1. Mary is 10 years old. She has a high fever of 39.5 °C.   [   ]
2. My grandfather has problems passing urine.   [   ]
3. I have a persistent abdominal pain.   [   ]
4. I have irregular periods.   [   ]
5. He fell over and sprained his ankle.   [   ]
6. I have a painful rash on my chest.   [   ]
7. I'm pregnant and expecting a baby soon.   [   ]
8. My father has problems with his heart.   [   ]

Chapter 6 | Medical Departments

Topic 2 Expressions for Medical Tests 検査のための表現

病気の診断には検査が欠かせません。手順はおおよそ決まっていますから、表現をしっかり覚えれば対応できます。

Q Fill in the blanks with the given words. 32

| breath | expose | fill | relax | fist | remove | collect | roll | have | change |

Blood test: 血液検査
① We're going to do a blood test.
② Please ¹(　　　) up your sleeve and put out your arm.
③ Please make a ²(　　　) with your thumb inside.
④ We're finished. ³(　　　) your hand.
⑤ Keep the pressure on the injection site for a few minutes.

Urine test: 尿検査
① You need to ⁴(　　　) a urine test.
② Here is a cup.
③ Urinate a small amount into the toilet, and then ⁵(　　　) the mid-stream sample in the cup.
④ ⁶(　　　) up about one third of the cup.

X-ray exam: 胸部レントゲン検査
① Please ⁷(　　　) into this hospital gown.
② Remove any metallic items.
③ Place your chin here.
④ Put your hands on your hips.
⑤ Take a deep ⁸(　　　) and hold it.
⑥ Please relax. We're all finished.

ECG test: 心電図
① Please ⁹(　　　) your socks.
② Please lie down on the exam table on your back.
③ Please ¹⁰(　　　) your chest.
④ I'll attach the ECG sensors.
⑤ Please relax.

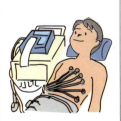

35

Medical Vocabulary — Body Systems 人体器官系

人体の組織・器官がどういう役割や機能を持っているかを知ることは、病気を診断したり、予見したりする上でとても大切です。まずどんな器官があるか英語表現を学びましょう。

- 消化器系： digestive system (esophagus, stomach, duodenum, colon etc.)
- 呼吸器系： respiratory system (pharynx, larynx, lungs, bronchus, etc.)
- 循環器系： cardiovascular system (heart, artery, vein, aorta, etc.)
- 内分泌系： endocrine system (thyroid, pancreas, adrenal gland, etc.)
- 筋骨格系： musculoskeletal system (skeleton, muscles, joints, etc.)
- 神経系： nervous system (brain, central NS, peripheral NS, spinal cord, etc.)
- 泌尿生殖器系： urogenital system (kidneys, bladder, uterus, testes, etc.)
- 外皮系： integumentary system (skin, hair and nails)

Q Label the numbers using the words (A – T).

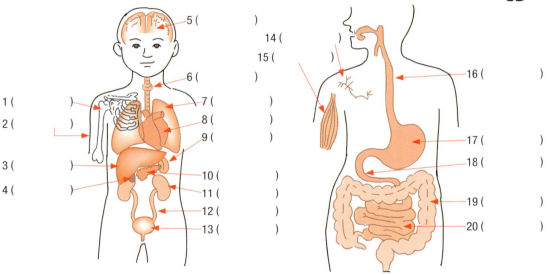

(A) lung	(B) bone	(C) kidney	(D) ureter	(E) spleen
(F) gall bladder	(G) brain	(H) esophagus	(I) skin	(J) duodenum
(K) nerve	(L) liver	(M) thyroid	(N) muscle	(O) large intestine
(P) stomach	(Q) bladder	(R) small intestine	(S) heart	(T) pancreas

One Point 看護情報

その略語の元ネタは？

臨床現場では「ウロ」「ギネ」などの略語（隠語）を耳にすることがあります。ウロは「urology（泌尿器科）」、「ギネ」は「gynecology（婦人科）」の略です。このような略語（隠語）の使用は推奨されませんが、覚えにくい診療科名を覚える手助けにはなるかもしれません。また、病棟によって使われ方が違う略語もあります。例えば「エピ」は麻酔科では、硬膜外ブロック（epidural block）、脳外科では、てんかん（epilepsy）を指していることがあります。ドイツ語由来の隠語も多いので、一度調べてみると勉強になるかもしれませんね。

Chapter 7

Review & Medical Terminology

まとめと
医学英語の構造

Chapter 1 から Chapter 6 で学んだ内容を復習しましょう。すべては積み重ねが大切です。外国人の患者さんとのコミュニケーションのために着実に覚えていきましょう。さらに、実際に病棟でよく使われる医学英語についてその構造を学びましょう。

Q1 Fill in the blanks with a word to match the Japanese.

1. 本日の担当看護師です。　　　　I'm your (　　　　　　) nurse today.
2. この病衣に着替えてください。　Please (　　　　　) (　　　　　　) this hospital gown.
3. このボタンを押して話してください。　(　　　　　　) this button and talk.
4. どうされましたか。　　　　　　What can I (　　　　　　) for you?
5. 血圧を測ってみましょう。　　　Let me (　　　　　　) your blood pressure.
6. マンシェットを巻きますね。　　I'll (　　　　　) this (　　　　　　) around your arm.
7. 脇の下に体温計を入れてください。　(　　　　　　) this thermometer (　　　　　) your arm.
8. 袖を捲ってください。　　　　　Please (　　　　　) (　　　　　　) your sleeve.

Q2 Put the words in the correct order.

1. いつ痛みが始まりましたか。　　　　did / when / pain / start / your / ?
2. どんな痛みか言えますか。　　　　　your / describe / you / pain / can / ?
3. その痛みはどのくらい続きましたか。　pain / long / how / the / last / did / ?
4. 正確にどこが痛いですか。　　　　　exactly / the / where / pain / is / ?
5. どのくらい痛いですか。　　　　　　you / would / pain / rate / how / your / ?
6. その症状はどのくらい続いていますか。　long / had / the symptom / you / how / have / ?
7. どんな症状がありますか。　　　　　symptoms / do / have / what / you / ?
8. 何回くらいこの症状が起きていますか。　times / this / many / happened / how / has / ?

37

Q3 Complete the crossword by filling in a word that fits each nursing item.

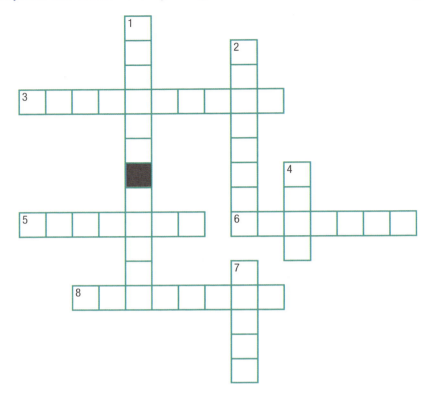

Across:

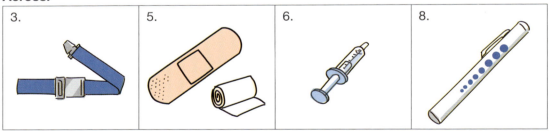

3. 5. 6. 8.

Down:

1. 2. 4. 7.

Chapter 7 Review & Medical Terminology

Q4 Fill in the blanks with the given symptoms.

| edema | dehydration | breath | rash | fever | itch | vomiting | loss of appetite |

1. When my son has an asthma attack, he has shortness of (   ).

2. You can prevent (   ) by drinking water regularly.

3. I don't feel like eating. (   ) can cause weight loss.

4. I'm afraid I have the flu. I have a/an (   ).

5. I was bit on the leg by a mosquito. I have a/an (   ).

6. Swelling in your feet is also called (   ).

7. I'm going to throw up. = I feel like (   ).

8. I'm allergic to crab. Look at the (   ) on my stomach.

Q5 Fill in the blanks with the given words to explain the illustrations.

| open | grab | bend | make | tiptoe | move |

1. (   ) your elbow.

2. (   ) your wrist.

3. (   ) your hand wide.

4. (   ) a fist.

5. Stand on (   ).

6. (   ) the handrail.

Q6 Mark T if the statement is true and F if it is not.

1. (　　) My baby has had diarrhea for three days. I'll take him to an endocrinologist.

2. (　　) You have been coughing for a week. You need to go to the pulmonology department.

3. (　　) My sister is having a baby. She visits the nephrology department.

4. (　　) I'm afraid my arm is broken. I want to go to dermatology.

5. (　　) I have persistent abdominal pain. I think I need to go see a gastroenterologist.

6. (　　) I have pain when I urinate. I want to see a urologist.

Q7 Find an organ to match the explanations.

kidneys	gall bladder	bladder	pancreas	esophagus

1. A hollow muscular organ that stores urine before expelling from the body.
[　　　　]

2. A small, pear-shaped muscular sac, located under the liver, in which bile secreted by the liver is stored. [　　　　]

3. A pair of organs located in the back of the abdomen which functions to filter the blood of metabolic wastes, which are then excreted as urine.
[　　　　]

4. It is a muscular tube connecting the throat (pharynx) with the stomach.
[　　　　]

5. It is a large gland located deep in the belly and is a vital part of the digestive system. It is a critical controller of blood sugar levels. [　　　　]

Chapter 7 | Review & Medical Terminology

Medical Terminology　医学英語の構造

　病棟内では、実に様々な医学英語の隠語や略語が使われています。たとえば「先生、患者さん、タキッてます」。これは、tachycardia「タキカーディア」(頻脈)の隠語です。医学英語の構造を知っていると、英語の病気名や処置などを推測して理解できるようになります。ここでは、医学英語の構造を学びます。

　医学単語は、単語の頭に付ける接頭辞 prefix、主に臓器名などの語根 root、語尾につける接尾辞 suffix という 3 つの要素に分けられます。それらは大抵、ギリシャ語およびラテン語から派生したものです。心電図 electrocardiogram を例にとって説明します。

> electrocardiogram は、electro + cardio + gram という 3 つの部分から出来ています。
> 　　　　　　　　　電気 ： 心臓 ： 記録
> 　　　　　　　　接頭辞 ： 語根 ： 接尾辞
> 　　　　　　　注)語根の後の (o) は発音がしやすいように入れられます。

1. 語根(root)には、語句の中心的なテーマや、臓器や器官名が来ます。

臓器・器官名		Root	臓器・器官		Root
脳	brain	encephalo-	目	eye	ophthalmo-
心臓	heart	cardio-	鼻	nose	rhino-
肺	lungs	pneumo-/pulmo-	耳	ear	oto-
肝臓	liver	hepato-	動脈	artery	arterio-
胃	stomach	gastro-	皮膚	skin	dermato-
腎臓	kidney	nephro-/reno-	骨	bone	osteo-
腸	intestine	entero-	血液	blood	hemo-
筋肉	muscle	myo-	神経	nerve	neuro-

2. 接頭辞(prefix)には、大きい、白い、悪い、高いなどの形容詞的な意味が来ます。

無い	an-	anemia	貧血
困難な	dys-	dyspnea	呼吸困難
白い	leuk-	leukemia	白血病
赤い	erythro-	erythrocyte	赤血球
高い	hyper-	hypertension	高血圧
低い	hypo-	hypothermia	低体温
悪い	mal-	malformation	形成不全
周辺	peri-	perinatal care	周産期ケア

41

3. 接尾語（suffix）には、状態、処置、症状などを表すものが来ます。

学問	-logy	urology	泌尿器学、泌尿器科
炎症	-itis	dermatitis	皮膚炎
切開	-tomy	tracheotomy	気管切開術
痛み	-algia	gastralgia	胃痛
麻痺	-plegia	quadriplegia	四肢麻痺
病	-pathy	neuropathy	神経障害
状態	-osis	osteoporosis	骨粗しょう症

Q1 Find a root word from the following medical terminology and match with the given organs. 35

| muscle | bone | nerve | liver | skin | ear | lung | kidney |

Medical Terminology	Organ
1. otitis media	
2. electromyogram	
3. neuralgia	
4. hepatitis	
5. dermatoma	
6. perinephritis	
7. ostectomy	
8. pneumonia	

Q2 Find an English medical term to match with the Japanese word keeping an eye on prefixes and suffixes. 36

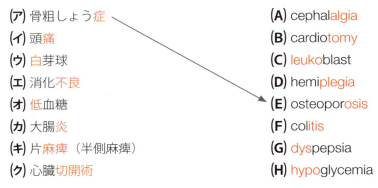

(ア) 骨粗しょう症　　　　　(A) cephalalgia
(イ) 頭痛　　　　　　　　　(B) cardiotomy
(ウ) 白芽球　　　　　　　　(C) leukoblast
(エ) 消化不良　　　　　　　(D) hemiplegia
(オ) 低血糖　　　　　　　　(E) osteoporosis
(カ) 大腸炎　　　　　　　　(F) colitis
(キ) 片麻痺（半側麻痺）　　(G) dyspepsia
(ク) 心臓切開術　　　　　　(H) hypoglycemia

Chapter 8

Personal Care

日常生活援助

日常生活援助は清潔保持だけでなく、全身の観察、日常生活活動（ADL）の評価、コミュニケーションの機会としても重要です。患者さんの羞恥心にも配慮しつつ、自分でできることは自分でやってもらえるように声をかけましょう。

Expressions to Remember   CD 37

Match the following Japanese expressions with the English ones below.

1. ベッド上で清拭をしますね。　_____
2. プライバシー確保のためにカーテンを閉めますね。　_____
3. この暖かい濡れタオルで顔を拭いてください。　_____
4. ベッドの高さを上げますね。　_____
5. ベッドの片側に体を寄せますね。　_____
6. 服を脱ぐのをお手伝いしますね。　_____
7. きつく拭いていませんか。　_____
8. おしもは、ご自分で拭きますか。　_____

- Wipe your face with this hot wet towel.
- I'll pull this curtain to provide privacy.
- I'll help you undress.
- I'll raise the height of the bed.
- I'll give you a bed bath now.
- Would you like to wipe your private parts by yourself?
- Am I rubbing you too hard?
- I'll roll you to one side.

First Watching of the Animation   WEB動画 DVD CD 38

▶ Watch the animation and answer the following questions.

1. Is the patient feeling better now?　　　　　　　　　　　　Yes.　No.
2. Can the patient take a shower by himself?　　　　　　　　Yes.　No.
3. Did the patient close the curtain?　　　　　　　　　　　　Yes.　No.
4. Are there two nurses working together to give a bed bath?　Yes.　No.
5. Did the patient wipe his private parts by himself?　　　　　Yes.　No.

43

Chapter 8 Scenario: Second Watching & Dictation  38

 Watch the animation again and fill in the blanks.

Nurse: Hi, Mr. Maalouf, how are you feeling now?
Patient: Oh, Nurse Yamada, I'm feeling much better today.
Nurse: I'm so glad to hear that. I'm wondering if I can give you ¹(_____) now.
Patient: A bed bath? Do you mean I can't take a shower by myself?
Nurse: No, you're ²(_____) for a while. You need to take a bath in bed.
Patient: Oh, is that so? That's disappointing. Well, then, I want a bed bath now.
Nurse: Good. Would you like to use the bedside commode first?
Patient: No. I don't need to.
Nurse: OK, let me wash my hands first. I'll close the curtain for you. Well, let's start. Please ³(_____) with this hot wet towel. Is it OK if I raise the height of the bed?
Patient: Yes, please.
Nurse: Now, let me pull back your blanket a little bit. ⁴(_____) to one side and wash your back. OK?
Patient: Yes.
Nurse: I'll place a towel under your back to keep the bed dry. ⁵(_____). Now I'm applying a hot wet towel. Am I ⁶(_____) too hard?
Patient: No, not at all. It feels so good.
Nurse: Now, I can move to your leg.
Patient: OK.
Nurse: Now, could you roll to ⁷(_____) if you can?
Patient: OK, like this?
Nurse: Good. I'll refill the basin with clean hot water. I'll wash your opposite side, too. Would you like to wipe ⁸(_____) by yourself?
Patient: Yes. Thank you.
Nurse: All done.

 Watch the animation again and practice with your partner.

44

Chapter 8 Personal Care

Comprehension Questions

Answer the following questions.

1. What does the nurse want to do now?
   (A) She wants to take the patient to the bathroom.
   (B) She wants to give the patient a bed bath.
   (C) She wants to change the patient's position.
   (D) She wants to give the patient a shower.

2. Why does the patient need a bed bath?
   (A) Because he didn't feel well.
   (B) Because he is going to have an operation.
   (C) Because he needs to be confined to bed.
   (D) Because he is unconscious.

3. What did the nurse do first before giving a bed bath?
   (A) She took off the patient's blanket.
   (B) She washed the patient's face.
   (C) She lowered the height of the bed.
   (D) She closed the curtain.

4. Which of the following is true?
   (A) The nurse wiped the patient's face.
   (B) The patient wanted to use the commode before a bed bath.
   (C) The patient wiped his face by himself.
   (D) The patient is unable to change his position.

5. Which of the following is true?
   (A) The nurse washed only one side of the patient's body at a time.
   (B) The nurse washed the patient's whole upper body first.
   (C) The nurse took away the blanket before giving a bed bath to the patient.
   (D) The nurse rubbed the patient very hard.

■◀ **Watch the animation again and try to play the nurse's role.**

45

FOCUS TOPICS

Topic 1 Personal Care Items 身だしなみ用具

採血や注射などを行う「診療の補助」の他に、食事や入浴、着衣などの日常生活活動（ADL: Activities of Daily Living）への援助である「療養上の世話」も看護師の大切な役割です。身の回りを整えるのに使う物品の英語名を覚えましょう。

Q Label the following personal care items using the given words. 39

tissues	scissors	bath towel	washbowl	comb	brush
pajamas	bobby pins	hand towel	mirror	hair dryer	razor
swabs	dentures	nail clippers	toothpaste & toothbrush		

1. (　　)
2. (　　)
3. (　　)
4. (　　)
5. (　　)
6. (　　)
7. (　　)
8. (　　)
9. (　　)
10. (　　)
11. (　　)
12. (　　)
13. (　　)
14. (　　)
15. (　　)
16. (　　)

Topic 2　Expressions for Personal Care　日常生活援助表現

日常生活活動（ADL）への援助の中でここでは、特に整容（着替え、洗面、歯みがき、整髪など）、及び食事の介助に使う表現を学びます。

Q1　Fill in the blanks with the given words. 40

| undo | zip | undress | pull | button | unzip |

着替え	Changing Clothes
• 服を脱ぐのをお手伝いします。 • ご自分でパジャマに着替えられますか。	• I'll help you ¹(　　　　　). • Can you put on your pajamas by yourself?
• ズボンを上げますね。 • ズボンを下ろしますね。	• I'll ²(　　　　　) up your pants. • I'll pull down your pants.
• ボタンをはずしますね。 • ボタンをはめますね。	• I'll ³(　　　　　) the buttons. • I'll do up the buttons. 　= I'll ⁴(　　　　　) your shirt.
• 上着のジッパーを上げますね。 • 上着のジッパーを下げますね。	• I'll ⁵(　　　　　) up your jacket. • I'll ⁶(　　　　　) your jacket.

Q2　Fill in the blanks with the given words. 41

| put | spit | brush | wipe | rinse | dentures |

身体整容、食事	Dental care, Hair Grooming, Feeding
• 歯を自分で磨けますか。 • 口をすすいでください。 • マウスリンスを吐き出してください。 • 入れ歯を洗いましょうか。	• Can you ¹(　　　　　) your teeth yourself? • ²(　　　　　) out your mouth. • ³(　　　　　) out the mouth rinse. • Shall I clean your ⁴(　　　　　)?
• 髪をとかしますね。 • 髪をまとめておきたいですか。	• I'll brush your hair. • Would you like to ⁵(　　　　　) your hair up?
• お食事のお手伝いしますね。 • どれから先に食べたいですか。 • お口をお拭きしますね。 • もう終わりましたか。	• I'll help you eat the meal. • Which food would you like to eat first? • I'll ⁶(　　　　　) your mouth. • Are you done eating?

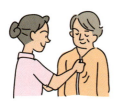  

Medical Vocabulary Interprofessional Team 専門家との連携

病院内の看護師にも一定のヒエラルキー (hierarchy) があります。各施設によって呼び方が異なりますが、基本的なものだけをここにはあげています。また、看護師は、多職種とお互いを尊重し合いながら協力して、患者さんを支援します。どんな職種があるでしょうか。

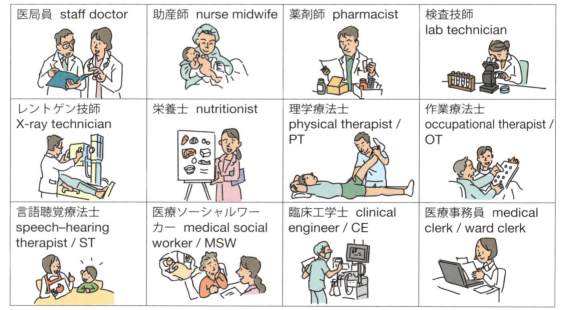

One Point 看護情報

高度実践看護師とは？

海外では、日本でいう看護師（Registered Nurse: RN）の資格に加え、大学院以上の教育を受け高度な専門知識を持って看護を実践する高度実践看護師（Advanced Practice Nurse: APN）という資格を設けているところがあります。近年、日本でも海外の APN に対応する看護師を育成するプログラムを整えようとする動きが活発になっています。医療現場のコミュニケーションだけでなく、制度もグローバル化が進んでいますね。

与薬

Giving Medication to a Patient

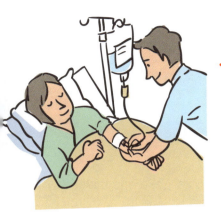

薬は正しく服用すれば薬になり、誤って服用すれば毒にもなります。5R つまり正しい患者さん（right patient）に、正しい薬（right drug）を、正しい量（right dose）で、正しい時間（right time and frequency of administration）に、正しい方法（right route）で服用してもらうための表現を身に付けましょう。

Expressions to Remember 43

Match the following Japanese expressions with the English ones below.

1. 1日3回毎食後1カプセルを飲んでください。 _____
2. この錠剤は動脈血栓を防ぎます。 _____
3. この錠剤は、便秘のためのものです。 _____
4. 必要に応じて1〜2錠飲んでください。 _____
5. このカプセルで便秘を起こすかもしれません。 _____
6. この処方箋を薬局で調剤してもらってください。 _____
7. この軟膏を1日数回塗ってください。 _____
8. 血が止まるまで押さえていてください。 _____

- Take one or two tablets as needed.
- These tablets are to prevent arterial clots.
- These capsules may make you constipated.
- Take one capsule three times a day after each meal.
- Please get the prescription filled at a pharmacy.
- Hold this until the bleeding stops.
- These tablets are for constipation.
- Apply this ointment several times a day.

First Watching of the Animation    44

▶ Watch the animation and answer the following questions.

1. Is the patient going to be discharged from the hospital?   Yes. No.
2. Does he need medicine for diabetes?   Yes. No.
3. Does he have regular bowel movements?   Yes. No.
4. Did he have cataract surgery?   Yes. No.
5. Will he receive the medicine at the hospital?   Yes. No.

Chapter 9 Scenario: Second Watching & Dictation   44

◀ Watch the animation again and fill in the blanks.

Nurse: Mr. Boonyasak, I'd like to show you how to take your medications now before your discharge. It's very important to take them regularly.
Patient: Oh, OK.
Nurse: These capsules are for your blood pressure. [1](   ) twice a day.
Patient: One capsule twice a day.
Nurse: Yes. And [2](   ) arterial clots. Take one tablet after every meal.
Patient: Got it.
Nurse: And these tablets [3](   ). Take one or two tablets [4](   ) a lot of water.
Patient: I have regular movements.
Nurse: Good. But these capsules for blood pressure [5](   ). You shouldn't strain on the toilet.
Patient: Oh, I understand.
Nurse: You also have eye drops for cataracts, don't you?
Patient: Yes, how often should I use them?
Nurse: Twice a day.
Patient: By the way, where can I get these medicines?
Nurse: You will receive a prescription at discharge. Please [6](   ) at any pharmacy. And this is an appointment card. Please keep your appointment.
Patient: Oh, I don't know if I can make it.
Nurse: Mr. Boonyasak, it's very important to keep your appointment. Your prescription [7](   ) and you need to have blood tests done.
Patient: Oh, is that so? OK. I will try to keep it.
Nurse: Good. Whenever you have problems such as shortness of breath, nausea, or persistent headache, [8](   ) to call us.
Patient: Sure. Thank you so much.

◀ Watch the animation again and practice with your partner.

Chapter 9 Giving Medication to a Patient

⟐ Comprehension Questions

Answer the following questions.

1. Why did the nurse come to the patient?
   (A) She wanted to talk about his bowel movements.
   (B) She wanted to explain about his medicines.
   (C) She wanted to explain about some side effects of his medicines.
   (D) She wanted to talk about his lifestyle after he is discharged from the hospital.

2. What are these capsules for?
   (A) blood pressure
   (B) arterial clots
   (C) constipation
   (D) cataracts

3. What side effects could he have from his medicines?
   (A) diarrhea
   (B) sleeplessness
   (C) irritability
   (D) constipation

4. Why does he need an eye solution?
   (A) He has cataracts.
   (B) He has a sty.
   (C) He has glaucoma.
   (D) He is near-sighted.

5. What else did the nurse give him?
   (A) a prescription
   (B) blood test results
   (C) an appointment card
   (D) a telephone card

▮◀ Watch the animation again and try to play the nurse's role.

51

FOCUS TOPICS

Topic 1 Types of Medication　薬剤の種類

看護師は、医師の指示のもとに注射をし、また、一人で薬を飲めない人への介助や、正しい服用を促し、副作用の観察などを行います。様々な薬剤を正しく英語で言えるようにしましょう。

Q1 Match the given words to the illustrations below. 45

| inhaler | ointment | suppository | IV drip | tablets | syrup |
| injection | capsules | eye drops | lozenges | powder | patch |

1. [　　　]
2. [　　　]
3. [　　　]
4. [　　　]
5. [　　　]
6. [　　　]
7. [　　　]
8. [　　　]
9. [　　　]
10. [　　　]
11. [　　　]
12. [　　　]

Q2 Fill in the names of medications in the above illustrations according to the categories.

Categories	Types of Medications		
oral dosage forms　経口薬	[tablets]	[　　　]	[　　　]
	[　　　]	[　　　]	
topical dosage forms　経皮薬	[　　　]	[　　　]	
rectal dosage forms　経腸薬	[　　　]		
inhaled dosage forms　吸入薬	[　　　]		
ophthalmic dosage forms　点眼薬	[　　　]		
parenteral dosage forms　非経口薬	[　　　]	[　　　]	

Chapter 9　Giving Medication to a Patient

Topic 2　Medication Instructions　投薬指示関連の表現

看護師は処方された通りに、患者さんが薬を服用できるようにしっかり指示する必要があります。医療事故を防ぐためにも表現をしっかり学びましょう。

 46

錠剤、カプセル	Tablets / Capsules
1日にどれだけ薬を飲めばいいのですか。	What is the daily dose?
1日3回毎食後2錠飲んでください。	Take two tablets three times a day after each meal.
寝る前に2カプセル飲んでください。	Take two capsules before bedtime.
必要な時には1カプセル飲んでください。	Take one capsule whenever needed.
たくさんの水と一緒に飲んでください。	Please take the medicine with plenty of water.
座薬	Suppository
高熱がある時には、座薬を1つ直腸に入れてください。	Insert one suppository into the rectum when you have a high fever.
軟膏	Ointment
この軟膏を1日数回塗ってください。	Apply this ointment several times a day.
目薬	Eye Drops
1日3回目薬を差してください。	Put in the eye drops three times a day.
注射、点滴	Injection / IV Drip
痛み止めを注射しますね。	I'll give you an injection of a painkiller.
筋肉注射をしますね。	I'll give you an intramuscular injection.
1分間しっかり押さえておいてください。	Press firmly for one minute.
点滴をしますね。	I'm going to give you an IV drip.
点滴は2時間ほどかかります。	The infusion will take about two hours.
トローチ剤	Lozenge
のど飴をゆっくり口の中で溶かしてください。	Dissolve one lozenge slowly in your mouth.
副作用	Side Effects
この薬は、副作用で吐き気を起こすかもしれません。	This medicine may make you nauseated as a side effect.
副作用には吐き気や嘔吐があります。	The side effects include nausea and vomiting.

53

Medical Vocabulary   Efficacy of Medicine   薬の効能

薬には様々な効能があります。今自分が飲んでいる薬にはどんな効能があるか知ることで、病気の治療に前向きとなり、さらに副作用の回避にもつながります。

 47

日本語	英語	効能
抗生剤	antibiotic	It destroys bacteria.
解熱剤	antipyretic	It reduces fever.
下剤	laxative	It promotes bowel movements.
下痢止め	antidiarrhetic	It stops diarrhea.
消化剤	digestant	It promotes digestion.
鎮静剤	sedative	It reduces irritability or excitement.
眠剤	sleeping pill	It induces sleep.
鎮痛剤	pain killer / analgesic	It eases pain.
抗高血圧薬	antihypertensive	It is used to treat hypertension.
利尿剤	diuretic	It promotes the increased production of urine.
気管支拡張剤	bronchodilator	It widens the air passages by relaxing the bronchial muscle.
消炎剤	anti-inflammatory	It reduces inflammation.
市販薬	over-the-counter drug OTC medicine	It is a medicine sold directly to you without a prescription from a doctor.

Q Fill in the blanks with the above medicine.

1. The patient has a fever above 104 °F (40 °C). He needs a/an (　　　　) immediately.
2. The patient's stools are frequent and watery. She needs a/an (　　　　).
3. My father has high blood pressure and he takes a/an (　　　　).
4. My child has asthma. Sometimes she wheezes when she breathes. She needs a/an (　　　　).
5. When you are constipated, you may need a/an (　　　　).

One Point 看護情報

コミュニケーションの新しい形

慢性疾患を持つ約17万人を対象とした研究[2]では、治療開始から1年後に、正しく薬を飲み続けている患者は3割前後に過ぎないことが示されています。正しく服薬をしてもらうための方法については、医療者による退院指導や電話を用いた支援の効果などが調べられてきました。最近では患者さんの携帯電話にリマインドメールを送ると適切な服薬行動が促されるとの報告[3]もあります。今後はスマートフォンのアプリや人工知能の発展も期待できるので、正しい服薬を促すための患者・医療者間のコミュニケーションの在り方も変わっていくかもしれません。

排泄（排便／排尿）

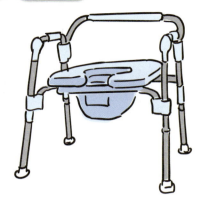

Elimination (Bowel Movement / Urination)

排泄は患者さんにとっては基本的欲求であり、医療者にとっては患者さんの消化器・泌尿器・循環器系等をアセスメントするための大切な情報でもあります。患者さんの尊厳を守りつつ、適切に情報を得るための表現を身に付けましょう。

Expressions to Remember

 48

Match the following Japanese expressions with the English ones below.

1. 昨日、排便は何回ありましたか。　_____
2. どのくらいの期間、下痢していますか。　_____
3. 今日は便が出ましたか。　_____
4. もう４日間、便秘をしているのですね。　_____
5. 最後に排便したのはいつですか。　_____
6. 昨日は、何回おしっこが出ましたか。　_____
7. 排尿時に痛みはありますか。　_____
8. 便器を腰の下に入れますね。　_____

- You've been constipated for four days now.
- I'll put the bedpan under you.
- Did your bowels move today?
- How many times did you have bowel movements yesterday?
- How many times did you urinate yesterday?
- When was your last bowel movement?
- How long have you had diarrhea?
- Do you have any pain during urination?

First Watching of the Animation

   49

▶ Watch the animation and answer the following questions.

1. Could the patient sleep well last night?　　Yes.　No.
2. Does he have constipation?　　Yes.　No.
3. Has he taken a laxative?　　Yes.　No.
4. Is he going to take a laxative?　　Yes.　No.
5. Does he have painful urination?　　Yes.　No.

55

Chapter 10 Scenario: Second Watching & Dictation   49

◀ Watch the animation again and fill in the blanks.

Nurse: Good morning, Mr. Whitney. Did you ¹(   ) last night?
Patient: Oh, Nurse Yoshida. No, I didn't.
Nurse: Why was that?
Patient: I felt bloated.
Nurse: Did you go to the bathroom?
Patient: Yes. I strained and pushed, but I couldn't.
Nurse: When did you last have a bowel movement?
Patient: I haven't had one since the operation.
Nurse: So, you have been constipated for four days. Have you ²(   )?
Patient: No, I usually have regular ³(   ). I just don't like to take medicine.
Nurse: You've been inactive since the operation, that may be the reason for the constipation. It'll take time to get back to ⁴(   ). I think laxatives will help your bloated stomach.
Patient: Oh, OK. I'll take one.
Nurse: I'll bring it soon. How about urination? ⁵(   ) did you urinate yesterday?
Patient: Yesterday? Well, five to six times, I think.
Nurse: Did you have any pain ⁶(   )?
Patient: No.
Nurse: How is your appetite? Did you eat breakfast this morning?
Patient: I've ⁷(   ). I ate only half of it.
Nurse: Try to drink more and eat ⁸(   ). I hope you'll recover your appetite when your constipation is gone.

◀ Watch the animation again and practice with your partner.

56

Chapter 10 Elimination (Bowel Movement / Urination)

⊠ Comprehension Questions

Answer the following questions.

1. Why is Mr. Whitney hospitalized?

(A) Because he has urinary problems.

(B) Because he doesn't have an appetite.

(C) Because he has problems emptying his bowels.

(D) Because he has undergone an operation.

2. How long has he been constipated?

(A) for three days

(B) for four days

(C) for five days

(D) for six days

3. How much breakfast did he eat this morning?

(A) He ate it all.

(B) He ate half of it.

(C) He ate one third of it.

(D) He couldn't eat at all.

4. Why hasn't he asked for laxatives?

(A) Because he doesn't like the taste of laxatives.

(B) Because he usually has constipation.

(C) Because he didn't know he could have laxatives.

(D) Because he doesn't like to take medicine.

5. What was the cause of his constipation that the nurse explained?

(A) inactiveness

(B) anesthesia

(C) medication he is taking now

(D) food he is having now

◀ **Watch the animation again and try to play the nurse's role.**

57

FOCUS TOPICS

Topic 1　Expressions for Elimination　排泄の表現

排尿、排便の話題はきわめてプライベートな部分であり、したがってプライバシーや自尊心への十分な配慮が必要です。どぎまぎしないで確認できるように、しっかり表現を覚えましょう。

 50

排便	Defecation
昨日、排便は何回ありましたか。	• How many times did you have a bowel movement yesterday? • How many times did you move your bowels yesterday?
排便はありましたか。 便は出ましたか。	• Did you have a bowel movement yesterday? • Did your bowels move today? • Did you pass stool today? • Did you have a motion today? • To a child: Did you do number 2?
3日前から便が出ていません。	I haven't had a bowel movement for three days.
便秘	Constipation
もう1週間も便秘をしています。	• I've been constipated for a week now. • I'm suffering from constipation this week.
下痢	Diarrhea
下痢をしています。	• I have diarrhea. • I've got the runs. • I have loose stools.
下痢をしていますか。	Have you got loose bowels?
どのくらいの期間下痢をしていますか。	How long have you had diarrhea?
検便	Stool Sample
検査のため検便をしてください。	You need to provide a stool sample for testing.
排尿	Urination
おしっこに行きたい。	• I have to pee. Where is the bathroom? • I want to pass water. • To a child: Do you have to go number 1?
昨日、何回おしっこが出ましたか。	How many times did you urinate yesterday?
尿検査のためにおしっこを取ってください。	Please collect a urine sample for a urinalysis.

58

Chapter 10 | Elimination (Bowel Movement / Urination)

Topic 2　What is the Urinary System?　排尿の仕組み

患者さんに病気の説明をする時には、臓器や組織がどんな仕事をしているか説明することもあります。ここでは、排尿の仕組みを英語で理解しましょう。

51

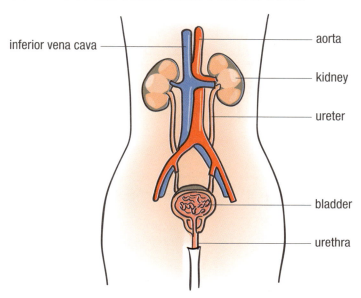

Q Fill in the blanks with the given words to find the function of the urinary system.

| ureters | blood | urethra | bottom | waste | bladder | urine | fist |

1. The main function of the urinary system is to get rid of ¹(　　　　) and extra fluid from the body.

2. The kidneys are two bean-shaped organs, each about the size of a ²(　　　　), located in the back of your abdomen under your lower ribs.

3. The kidneys filter extra water and wastes out of your ³(　　　　) and make urine.

4. The urine flows from the kidneys to the ⁴(　　　　) through two thin tubes of muscle called ⁵(　　　　), one on each side of the bladder.

5. The bladder stores ⁶(　　　　) until you are ready to go to the bathroom to empty it.

6. When the bladder empties, urine flows out of the body through a tube called the ⁷(　　　　), located at the ⁸(　　　　) of the bladder.

59

Medical Vocabulary

Bowel and Urinary Elimination
排便、排尿にかかわる語彙

排便、排尿に関わる物品や症状を取り上げます。 52

便	Stool	尿	Urine
差し込み便器	bedpan	しびん	urinal
室内便器（カモード）	commode	膀胱内留置カテーテル 蓄尿バッグ	Foley catheter urine drainage bag
おむつ	diaper		
排便	bowel movement	排尿障害	dysuria, problem with urinating
下痢	diarrhea	尿意切迫	urinary urgency
便秘	constipation	頻尿	urinary frequency, frequent urination
血便　タール便	bloody stool / tarry stool	過活動膀胱	overactive bladder (OAB)
下剤	laxative	血尿	hematuria
消化不良	indigestion	尿失禁	urinary incontinence
腹部膨満	bloating	尿路感染	urinary tract infection (UTI)
嚥下困難	dysphasia, difficulty in swallowing	尿閉	urinary retention
食欲不振	loss of appetite	タンパク尿	proteinuria
人工肛門	stoma and ostomy	残尿感	residual urine

One Point 看護情報

WOC（ウォック）看護師

看護現場における看護ケアの広がりと質の向上をはかることを目的として、熟練した看護技術と知識を用いて水準の高い看護実践を行う看護師を育成する認定看護師制度があります。その一分野に、皮膚・排泄ケア (Wound, Ostomy and Continence Nursing) があり、通称 WOC 看護師と呼ばれています。褥瘡（じょくそう）などの創傷管理の他に、ストーマ管理や排尿の自立支援などを行う分野です。人種を超えて、人間の営みの中で大切な部分に対する援助です。

Chapter 11

慢性疾患

Chronic Diseases

長い経過をたどる慢性疾患は、患者さんの生活に密着しています。症状や治療だけでなく、食生活や運動習慣、家庭環境など、生活全体をアセスメントしていきましょう。

Expressions to Remember　　53

Match the following Japanese expressions with the English ones below.

1. 今回の入院についてお聞きしたいと思います。
2. どんな症状でしょうか。
3. 血液中の余分な水分で足のむくみが起きます。
4. 日常の食事についてお話しください。
5. 食事中の塩分に気をつけているのですね。
6. お酒を飲んだりタバコなどを吸っていますか。
7. 家族の中に心不全と診断された方はいますか。
8. 健康維持のために何かしていますか。

- What symptoms do you have?
- You're watching sodium in your diet.
- What do you do to stay healthy?
- Is there anyone in your family who has been diagnosed with heart failure?
- I would like to ask you a few things about your hospitalization.
- Do you drink alcohol or smoke cigarettes?
- Excess fluids in the blood cause swelling in the feet.
- Could you tell me about your daily diet?

First Watching of the Animation　　54

Watch the animation and determine if each statement is True or False.

1. The patient's family recommended hospitalization to him.　　True　False
2. The patient gained 3 kg in two weeks.　　True　False
3. The patient has difficulty breathing during rest.　　True　False
4. The patient sleeps well at night.　　True　False
5. The patient stopped smoking.　　True　False

Chapter 11 Scenario: Second Watching & Dictation

◀ Watch the animation again and fill in the blanks.

Nurse: Hello, Mr. Mendoza. I'm Nurse Suzuki, your primary nurse. I would like to ask you a few things about your hospitalization today. Is that OK?

Patient: Yes.

Nurse: Could you tell me why you ¹(　　　　　　　　　　　　)?

Patient: The doctor says my heart condition is getting worse. He recommended hospitalization.

Nurse: ²(　　　　　　　　　　　　) do you have?

Patient: I feel difficulty breathing while exercising. I'm usually OK at rest though. I notice swelling in my feet. I also have gained 3 kg in two weeks, even though I haven't eaten much.

Nurse: May I ³(　　　　　　　　　　　　) now?

Patient: Yes, go ahead.

Nurse: Thank you. Well, when the heart is not working well, fluids in the blood tend to build up in the tissues and ⁴(　　　　　　　　　　　　) in the feet and ⁵(　　　　　　　　　　　　). Can you sleep well at night?

Patient: I feel suffocated and wake up in the middle of the night.

Nurse: Is that so? Could you tell me about your daily diet?

Patient: I have been trying to follow a diet low in sodium as recommended. But I live alone and often have take-out lunches. I'm not sure if I'm doing well or not.

Nurse: You're watching your sodium. Wonderful! ⁶(　　　　　　　　　　　　)?

Patient: I used to, but ever since I was diagnosed with heart failure, I quit smoking.

Nurse: Good for you. How about drinking alcohol?

Patient: I drink two to three times a week. But just a little.

Nurse: What and how much do you drink?

Patient: Just a can of beer.

Nurse: Is there anyone ⁷(　　　　　　　　　　　　) who has been diagnosed with heart failure?

Patient: My father died of ⁸(　　　　　　　　　　　　) at the age of 65.

Nurse: Thank you very much. That's all for now. I'll come back to take your vital signs in 20 minutes.

◀ Watch the animation again and practice with your partner.

Chapter 11 Chronic Diseases

⏩ Comprehension Questions

Answer the following questions

1. Why is the patient hospitalized?
   (A) Because he has been suffocated.
   (B) Because his heart condition is getting worse.
   (C) Because he has swollen feet.
   (D) Because he has a sleeping problem.

2. Which of the following is NOT true?
   (A) He drinks alcohol.
   (B) He lost some weight.
   (C) His feet are swollen.
   (D) He doesn't smoke.

3. What information did he give about his daily diet?
   (A) He has a low-sodium diet.
   (B) He often cooks for himself.
   (C) He tends to eat too much.
   (D) He tries not to gain weight.

4. What information did the nurse want to know?
   (A) his activity levels
   (B) his elimination patterns
   (C) his value-belief patterns
   (D) his family medical history

5. What information did the nurse get about his family medical history?
   (A) He drinks a can of beer two to three times a week.
   (B) He can tell her the reason for his hospitalization.
   (C) His father died of a heart attack at the age of 65.
   (D) He wakes up in the middle of the night feeling suffocated.

🔲◀ **Watch the animation again and try to play the nurse's role.**

FOCUS TOPICS

Topic 1 Getting Patient Information 患者情報収集

一見医療とは関係の無いような患者さんの職歴や家庭環境なども、患者さんの健康状態を左右する重要な要素となっているケースが少なくありません。患者さんの機能的健康パターン（Functional Health Pattern）を知るために、しっかり情報収集をしましょう。

Q Fill in the blanks with the given words.   55

medicines	illnesses	occupation	allergies	exercise
operation	family	appetite	rested	alcohol

既往歴 • 過去に重大な病気をしたことはありますか。 • 入院したことはありますか。 • 手術を受けたことはありますか。	**Medical History** • Have you ever had any serious [1](　　　) in the past? • Have you ever been hospitalized before? • Have you had an [2](　　　) before?
服薬 • 何か薬を服用していますか。	**Medication** • Are you taking any [3](　　　)? • Are you taking any medication?
アレルギー • アレルギーはありますか。 • 何かにアレルギーはありますか。	**Allergy** • Do you have any [4](　　　)? • Are you allergic to anything?
飲酒喫煙 • 飲酒喫煙はされますか。 • どれくらい飲まれますか。	**Alcohol Intake / Use of Tobacco** • Do you drink [5](　　　) or smoke cigarettes? • How much do you drink?
家族歴 • 家族で重い病気になった人はいますか。 • 家族に同じような病気になった人はいますか。	**Family History** • Are there any serious illnesses in your [6](　　　)? • Has anyone in your family had the same illness?
社会歴 • ご職業をお聞きしてもいいですか。 • ご結婚されていますか。 • 家族は近くに住んでいますか。 • どなたと暮らしていますか。	**Social History** • May I ask what your [7](　　　) is? • Are you married? • Does your family live close by? • Who do you live with?
栄養・食事習慣 • 健康的に食べていらっしゃいますか。 • 食欲はありますか。	**Nutritional-Metabolic** • Do you think you are a healthy eater? • How is your [8](　　　)?

運動習慣	Activity-Exercise
• 1週間にどれほど運動されますか。 • 空き時間には何をされていますか。	• How much [9]( ) do you get in a week? • What do you like to do in your spare time?
睡眠、休息	Sleep-Rest
• 気持ちよく目覚められますか。 • 夜はよく眠れますか。	• Do you feel [10]( ) when you wake up? • Can you sleep well at night?

Topic 2　What are Chronic Diseases?　慢性病とは？

慢性病とはどういう病気でしょうか。どのような原因因子があるのでしょうか。慢性病と診断された患者さんに、慢性病について正しく説明できますか。

Q Fill in the blanks using the given words or choose the best word.

death　eating　weight　medication　risk　activity　tobacco　vaccines

1. Chronic diseases—including heart disease, stroke, and diabetes,—generally cannot be prevented by [1](   ) or cured by [2](   ), nor do they just disappear.

2. Chronic diseases are by far the leading cause of [3](   ) in the world, representing 70% of all deaths.

3. The causes of the main chronic diseases are well known. The most important [4](   ) factors are lifestyle related habits:
   • lack of physical [5](   )
   • poor [6](   ) habits
   • [7](   ) use
   • drinking too much alcohol

4. That is why chronic diseases are often called lifestyle-related diseases. What is a Japanese word for "lifestyle-related diseases"?
   (   )

5. Changes in diet that may be helpful in reducing the risk of chronic diseases include eating a diet that is *low / high / narrow* in fat and sugars and *poor / rich / high* in fruits, vegetables and wholegrain foods.

6. Obesity is a risk factor for a variety of chronic diseases. Following a healthy, balanced diet can help you to maintain a healthy [8](   ), lower your cholesterol and reduce your risk for chronic diseases.

65

Medical Vocabulary　List of Chronic Diseases　慢性疾患

様々な慢性疾患があります。ここでは一部をあげます。よく見られる病気ばかりですからしっかり覚えましょう。

 56

10大慢性病	10 Major Chronic Diseases
1. 高血圧	hypertension / high blood pressure
2. 冠動脈心疾患	coronary heart disease (CHD)
3. 肝炎	hepatitis
4. 脳卒中	stroke
5. がん	cancer
6. 喘息	asthma
7. 糖尿病	diabetes
8. 関節炎	arthritis
9. 慢性閉塞性肺疾患	chronic obstructive pulmonary disease (COPD)
10. 慢性腎疾患	chronic kidney disease
その他の慢性病	Other Chronic Diseases
肥満	obesity
てんかん	epilepsy
骨粗しょう症	osteoporosis
血友病	hemophilia

Q Fill in the blanks with the chronic diseases above.

1. (　　　　　) is a long-term lung disease that inflames and narrows the airways.
2. (　　　　　) is a joint disorder featuring inflammation.
3. (　　　　　) happens when your coronary arteries get narrower and reduce the blood flow to the heart.
4. (　　　　　) weakens bone and increases risk of bones breaking.
5. (　　　　　) is a group of neurological disorders characterized by recurrent seizures.

One Point 看護情報

「聴く力」を高める

英語を用いたコミュニケーションでは自分が言いたいことを相手に適切に伝えられるかという「話す力」に目が行きがちですが、慢性疾患を持つ方の支援で本当に大切なのは、相手を理解し、相手に自分で解決策を考えてもらうための「聴く力」です。P.18のコラムで紹介した共感的態度を示す表現に加え、「今、一番お困りのことはなんですか？」What is the biggest concern in your life? や「健康のために普段から気をつけていることはなんですか？」What do you do to stay fit? などのオープンクエスチョンを使って、相手への理解を深めながら、必要な看護を考えていくようにしましょう。

Chapter 12

Critical Care / Operating Room

急性期／手術室

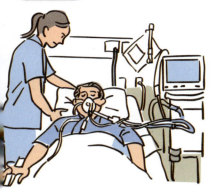

手術は人生の一大事です。ましてや、異国での手術はどんなに不安でしょうか。手術を受ける決心をした患者さんやご家族の思いを尊重しながら、手術を安全かつ確実に受けられるよう援助しましょう。

Expressions to Remember 57

Match the following Japanese expressions with the English ones below.

1. 病院の中では、このリストバンドを付けてください。　_____
2. 全身麻酔で手術は行われます。　_____
3. 気管チューブは手術後すぐ外されます。　_____
4. 弾性ストッキングは血液凝固を予防します。　_____
5. 今夜9時から、絶飲食です。　_____
6. 医師が眠剤を処方しています。　_____

- Your surgery will be performed under general anesthesia.
- Your breathing tube will be removed soon after the surgery.
- Compression stockings will prevent blood clots.
- Your doctor has prescribed a sleeping pill.
- Please wear this wristband during your stay in the hospital.
- You shouldn't eat or drink after 9 p.m. tonight.

First Watching of the Animation   58

🎬 Watch the animation and determine if each statement is True or False.

1. Nurse Yamada is a floor nurse.	True	False
2. Mrs. Miller is going to have an operation today.	True	False
3. She will have local anesthesia.	True	False
4. An anesthesiologist has come to explain about her anesthesia.	True	False
5. Mrs. Miller can take a sleeping pill.	True	False

67

Chapter 12 Scenario: Second Watching & Dictation

◀ Watch the animation again and fill in the blanks.

Nurse: Mrs. Miller? I'm Nurse Yamada, ¹( ).
I'll be there for your operation tomorrow.

Patient: Oh, nurse. I'm glad you've come to talk about it. I'm a bit anxious about it.

Nurse: ²( )?

Patient: Yes, please.

Nurse: Your surgery ³( ) under general anesthesia. You won't feel any pain.

Patient: An anesthesiologist came to me this morning and explained about a type of anesthesia.

Nurse: Good. After the surgery, you may need to go to the ICU depending ⁴( ). Your breathing tube will be removed soon after the surgery. When it is removed, ⁵( ) is necessary to prevent pneumonia. Can you do that?

Patient: (cough, cough) Like this?

Nurse: Much harder, please! (COUGH, COUGH)

Patient: (COUGH, COUGH)

Nurse: Good.

Patient: But why?

Nurse: It helps flush fluid ⁶( ). The compression stockings on your legs will be removed soon after you start walking.

Patient: Compression stockings?

Nurse: Yes, they will prevent blood clots during the surgery. And from 9 p.m. tonight, you shouldn't eat or drink to prevent the chance of vomiting and choking ⁷( ).

Patient: Oh, I see. But I don't think I can sleep tonight.

Nurse: Your doctor has prescribed a sleeping pill. Take this if necessary.

Patient: Oh, thank you.

Nurse: Do you have any questions about the surgery?

Patient: I would like to know how long the surgery will take.

Nurse: Normally it will take four to five hours. Anything else?

Patient: Not right now, thanks.

Nurse: Then, see you tomorrow at 7 a.m. Have ⁸( ).

◀ Watch the animation again and practice with your partner.

Chapter 12 | Critical Care / Operating Room

▶◀ Comprehension Questions

Answer the following questions.

1. Why did Nurse Yamada come to the patient?
  (A) She wanted to talk about the patient's sleeping patterns.
  (B) She wanted to give her a prescription.
  (C) She wanted to talk about the operation the next day.
  (D) She wanted to talk about the types of anesthesia.

2. Why is coughing and deep breathing necessary?
  (A) to prevent blood clots
  (B) to prevent sleeplessness
  (C) to improve blood circulation
  (D) to prevent pneumonia

3. What can't Mrs. Miller do after 9 p.m. before the surgery?
  (A) She can't cough.
  (B) She can't eat or drink.
  (C) She can't take a sleeping pill.
  (D) She can't wear compression stockings.

4. Which of the following is NOT true?
  (A) The patient will surely go to the ICU after the surgery.
  (B) The patient will wear compression stockings during surgery.
  (C) The patient is worried about the surgery.
  (D) Coughing helps clear the airways of lung irritants.

5. How long will the surgery take?
  (A) two to three hours
  (B) three to four hours
  (C) four to five hours
  (D) five to six hours

■◀ **Watch the animation again and try to play the nurse's role.**

FOCUS TOPICS

Topic 1 In the Emergency Room 救急室で

時間外や緊急に救急室を訪れる患者さんや患者家族に必ずしていただく手続きや質問です。しっかり覚えましょう。

1. At the ER 救急室で

Q1 Fill in the blanks with the given words.

available	fill
contact	wear

 59

この書類に記入してください。	Could you fill in this form?
この問診票に記入してください。	Could you [1]( ) out this questionnaire?
緊急の時に連絡できる方の名前を書いてください。	Could you write down the name of someone to [2]( ) in case of emergency?
今日はどうされましたか。	What brings you here today?
病院にいる間は、このリストバンドを付けていてください。	Please [3]( ) this wristband during your stay in the hospital.
医師の準備ができるまで待合室で座っていていただけますか。	Can you sit in the waiting room for a while until a doctor is [4]( )?
最も重病や重症の患者さんを優先的に診察します。	We will see the most seriously ill or injured first.

2. Orientation 見当識

見当識とは患者さんの意識レベルの1つで現在の時刻、日付、場所、人物、周囲の状況など、自分が今置かれている状況を理解する能力を意味します。救急室に運び込まれた患者さんの意識レベルを確認するために必ず聞く質問です。また、これらの理解能力が欠如することを失見当識（disorientation）と言います。

Q2 Fill in the blanks with the given words.

what	full
where	date

 60

患者の見当識	Patient's Orientation
名前を教えてください。	• Can you tell me your [1]( ) name, please? • May I have your name, please?
今は何年ですか。	[2]( ) year is it right now?
今日の日付はなんですか。	What is today's [3]( )?
今どこにいるか教えてください。	Can you tell me [4]( ) you are right now?

Chapter 12 Critical Care / Operating Room

Topic 2 Perioperative Care 周手術期看護

手術前（preoperative）、手術中（intraoperative）、手術後（postoperative）といった一連の期間における看護を周手術期看護と言います。手術室で働く看護師には、2つの役割があります。
- 器械出し看護師あるいは手洗い看護師（scrub nurse）は手術で使用する器械を事前に準備し、手術中は医師に器械を手渡します。
- 外回り看護師 (circulating nurse) は手術室全体に目を配り、患者の状態の観察、器械や薬剤の補充、手術の記録など手術を間接的にサポートします。

ここでは、外来手術の時によく使う表現を学びます。

Q Fill in the blanks with the given words. 61

| prevent | curled | breath | restroom | pressure |
| completed | remove | numb | permitted | condition |

術前指示	Instructing Your Patients before Surgery
処置の前におトイレを使ってください。	Please use the ¹(　　　　) before the procedure.
宝石やアクセサリーを外してください。	²(　　　　) all jewelry and accessories.
手術台に乗ってください。	Please get on the operating table.
マスクを着けますね。ゆっくり深呼吸してください。	I'll apply a mask. Take a deep ³(　　　　) slowly.
膝を胸の方に曲げるようにして横になってください。	Please lie on your side with your knees ⁴(　　　　) up towards your chest.
背中に注射をします。押される感じがすると思います。	Your doctor will give you an injection in your back. You may feel ⁵(　　　　).
痛んだり、しびれるようだったら教えてください。	If you have a pain or you feel ⁶(　　　　), let us know.
術後	After Surgery
娘さんの手術は終わりました。	Your daughter's surgery has been ⁷(　　　　).
お一人のご家族だけが回復室に入れます。	Only one family member will be ⁸(　　　　) to enter the recovery room.
娘さんの状態は、安定しています。	Your daughter's ⁹(　　　　) is stable.
まだ、うとうとしているかもしれません。	She may still be drowsy.
お手伝いしますから、起きて、動きましょう。血栓を予防できます。	I want to help you get up and move about now. It will ¹⁰(　　　　) blood clots.

71

Medical Vocabulary　ICU Glossary　集中治療室用語

ICUでよく使われる語彙を取り上げます。

トリアージ	triage
心肺停止	cardiopulmonary arrest (CPA)
心肺蘇生術	cardiopulmonary resuscitation (CPR)
対光反射	light reflex
痙攣（けいれん）	convulsion / seizure
輸血	blood transfusion
水分出納	intake & output
人工呼吸器	ventilator
経皮的心肺補助装置	percutaneous cardiopulmonary support (PCPS)
昏睡状態	coma

Q　Fill in the blanks with the given words.

seizure	triage	coma	CPR	CPA	ventilator	blood transfusion

1. The use of (　　　) means patients are attended to according to medical need and urgency.
2. The patient was brought to our emergency room. His breathing or heartbeat has stopped. The patient needed (　　　).
3. My son is having a (　　　). His body stiffens, jerks, and shakes, and he has lost consciousness.
4. Your daughter may need a (　　　). She is bleeding heavily because of an injury.
5. Your son has been unconscious and in a (　　　) since he was hit by a car.
6. Your husband is placed on a (　　　) now because he cannot breathe well enough on his own.

One Point 看護情報

非言語的コミュニケーション

救急や災害の現場で働く看護師さんから、倒れている患者さんの手を握る時、相手の手の上に自分の手を乗せるのではなく、相手の手の下に自分の手を入れて握るようにしていると伺ったことがあります。そうすることで、患者さんに「押さえつけられている」という印象を与えることを避け、安心感を与えられるとのことでした。見習いたい非言語的コミュニケーションです。

妊婦健診

Pregnancy Check-up

妊娠、出産に関する文化や慣習は、国によって違うでしょう。また、国によって医療のスタンダードも違います。丁寧に、日本での出産に向けた準備を説明する必要があります。英語による問診票、Check sheet などを事前に準備し、妊婦さんに寄り添いましょう。

❖ Expressions to Remember

Match these Japanese expressions with the English ones below.

1. 最後の生理はいつでしたか。
2. 妊娠 8 週ですよ。
3. 予定日は 12 月 12 日です。
4. 初めての妊娠ですか。
5. 流産や中絶したことはありますか。
6. 4 週ごとに、検査に来てください。
7. 採血しますね。
8. 袖をまくって、腕を出してください。

- Have you ever had an abortion or miscarriage?
- You're eight weeks pregnant.
- Roll up your sleeve and give me your arm, please.
- When was your last period?
- Is this your first pregnancy?
- Your due date is December 12th.
- I'd like to take your blood sample.
- Please come in for a check-up every four weeks.

◯ First Watching of the Animation WEB動画   64

▶ Watch the animation and determine if each statement is True or False.

1. Ms. Moraes missed her period last month.   **True False**
2. The nurse midwife will perform a transvaginal scan.   **True False**
3. Ms. Moraes is expecting a baby.   **True False**
4. Ms. Moraes needs to come back every three weeks.   **True False**
5. The nurse midwife will perform a urine test.   **True False**

Chapter 13 Scenario: Second Watching & Dictation  64

◀ Watch the animation again and fill in the blanks.

Nurse Midwife (N.M.): Ms. Moraes, when was your last period?
Ms. Moraes: It was March 5th. I ¹(   ) last month.
  N.M: OK, Dr. Kaneko will perform a transvaginal scan now. Please take off your underwear ²(   ) and get on the exam table. Please lie down on your back and ³(   ). And relax, OK?

(Some time later)

  N.M: Ms. Moraes, you're eight weeks pregnant. Your due date is December 10th. This is a pregnancy notification form. Please ⁴(   ) to the city office.
Ms. Moraes: Oh, am I? Wow, how wonderful!
  N.M: Ms. Moraes, have you ever had an abortion or miscarriage?
Ms. Moraes: Never.
  N.M.: So, this is your first pregnancy.
Ms. Moraes: Yes, it is.
  N.M: Do you smoke or drink?
Ms. Moraes: No, I don't.
  N.M: Good! Smoking and drinking alcohol cause serious complications during pregnancy. Well, Ms. Moraes, this is ⁵(   ). Please come in for a check-up every four weeks until 23 weeks.
Ms. Moraes: For a check-up? What do you do for a check-up?
  N.M: We'll check your urine and blood pressure. We'll also measure your weight, abdomen and fundal height, listen to ⁶(   ) and check the ⁷(   ) of the fetus.
Ms. Moraes: Oh, I understand.
  N.M: Today, I'd like to take a blood sample to check ⁸(   ), check your HIV, Hepatitis B, and syphilis status, and also check your immunity to rubella.

◀ Watch the animation again and practice with your partner.

74

Chapter 13 Pregnancy Check-up

◄► Comprehension Questions

Answer the following questions.

1. What is the nurse midwife going to do?

    (A) She is going to test Ms. Moraes's urine.

    (B) She is going to take Ms. Moraes's blood pressure.

    (C) She is going to take Ms. Moraes's blood sample.

    (D) She is going to listen to the fetal heartbeat.

2. When will Ms. Moraes visit this clinic next time?

    (A) in one week

    (B) in two weeks

    (C) in three weeks

    (D) in four weeks

3. When is Ms. Moraes's baby due?

    (   )

4. What will the nurse midwife measure at each check-up?

    (   ) (   ) (   )

5. What did the nurse midwife give to Ms. Moraes?

    (   ) and (   )

6. What will Ms. Moraes send in to the city office?

    (   )

7. Why shouldn't Ms. Moraes smoke or drink?

    Because smoking and drinking alcohol may (   ).

■◄ Watch the animation again and try to play the nurse's role.

FOCUS TOPICS

Topic 1 **First & Second Trimester** 妊娠初期・中期

母児ともに健康な妊娠期を過ごすことが正常な出産につながります。標準的な妊婦健診を説明できるようになりましょう。

Q Fill in the blanks with the given words. 65

| swelling | uterus | baby | protein | bowel | stress | weight | sugar |

尿中のタンパクと糖の値を調べます。	We'll test the ¹( ) and ²( ) levels in your urine.
腹囲、子宮底長を測定します。	I will measure your abdomen and the height of your ³( ).
足に浮腫があるか調べます。	We'll check your legs for ⁴( ).
ストレスをできるだけ少なくしましょう。	Minimize ⁵( ) in your life.
足を上げて休むと楽ですよ。	Resting with your legs elevated can be helpful.
便通は定期的にありますか。	Do you have regular ⁶( ) movements?
胎動はもう感じましたか。	Have you felt your ⁷( ) move yet?
過剰な体重増加は良くありません。	Excess ⁸( ) is not good.

What to Pack for Hospital: 病院への持ち物

- Hospital ID card：診察券
- Hospital admission form：入院手続き書類
- Health insurance card：保険証
- Mother & child health handbook：母子手帳
- Clothes to wear home：家に帰る時の服装
- Toiletries (toothbrush, toothpaste, makeup, hairbrush, shampoo, soap, lotion, hair dryer, etc.)：洗面用具（歯ブラシ、練り歯磨き、化粧品、ブラシ、シャンプー、石鹸、ローション、ドライヤーなど）
- Face towels and bath towels：タオル、バスタオル
- Slippers：スリッパ
- Chopsticks, cup：箸、コップ
- A box of tissues：ティッシュペーパー
- Pajamas (opening from the front)：パジャマ
- Underwear for lochia (postnatal discharge)：生理用パンティー
- Sanitary pads：生理ナプキン
- Two or more nursing bras：授乳用のブラ

For your baby to go home in:
- baby clothes　赤ちゃんの衣類
- newborn diapers　赤ちゃん用のおむつ

Chapter 13　Pregnancy Check-up

Topic 2　Labor & Delivery　陣痛と出産

本物の陣痛（labor contraction）のタイミングを掴むのは、簡単ではないようです。妊婦さんから「陣痛が始まったのではないか」と連絡が入ったら、落ち着いて、以下の項目を確認します。

Q Put the words in the correct order. 66

1. 予定日はいつですか。　　　　　　　When / due / your / is / date / ?
2. 妊娠何週ですか。　　　　　　　　　How / are / weeks / many / pregnant / you / ?
3. 収縮はどれくらいおきですか。　　　How / are / often / the contractions / ?
4. どれくらい続きますか。　　　　　　How / does / last / each contraction / long / ?
5. 痛みの強さはどれくらいですか。　　How / the contractions / are / painful / ?
6. 陣痛の間隔はどれくらいですか。　　How / are / apart / far / your contractions / ?
7. 破水しましたか。　　　　　　　　　/ broken / have / your / waters / ?
8. 陣痛が始まったようですね。　　　　/ like / started / your / has / sounds / it / labor / .

At a hospital or birth center: 67

赤ちゃんがどれくらい下がってきたか調べますね。	Let me see how far down your baby has come.
子宮口はまだ十分開大していませんよ。	Your cervix is not fully dilated yet.
分娩室にお連れしますね。	I'll take you to the delivery room.
帝王切開が必要になります。	You need a C-section.
息が続くかぎりいきんでください。	Now push as long as you can!
赤ちゃんの頭が見えてきました。	I can see your baby's head.
ハアハアして。	Keep panting!
ほら、赤ちゃんですよ。	Here is your baby.

77

Medical Vocabulary Midwifery Glossary 産科用語

婦人科や産科で使われる語彙を学びます。

Q1 Label the numbers with the given words. 68

| ovary | cervix | uterine tube | uterus | vagina |

Female Reproduction System

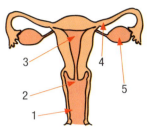

1. (	)	膣
2. (	)	頸部
3. (	)	子宮
4. (	)	卵管
5. (	)	卵巣

Q2 Label the numbers with the given Japanese words. 69

| 子宮壁 | 羊水 | 臍帯 | 胎児 | 胎盤 |

Fetus in the Uterus

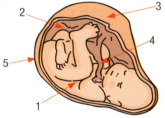

1. fetus	(	)
2. amniotic fluid	(	)
3. placenta	(	)
4. umbilical cord	(	)
5. uterine wall	(	)

その他の語彙： 70

おしるし	bloody show	臨月	full term
帝王切開	Cesarean section	陣痛	labor pain
硬膜外麻酔	epidural anesthesia	前置胎盤	placenta previa
胎動	fetal movement	早期産児	preterm infant

One Point 看護情報

誇るべき母子手帳

母子手帳 (Mother & child health handbook) は、妊娠・出産・子どもの健康記録が一冊にまとめられ、母子が共に継続ケアを受けるための健康記録です。戦後、復興のさなかにあった日本で 1948 年に作られた、日本発祥の誇るべきシステムです。今では世界の約 40 ヵ国に広がっているそうです。

2015 年秋、ウェブメディアや SNS を通じて、難民のかばんの中身を紹介した写真が話題になりました[(4)]。その中の 1 枚に写っていたのは、ビニール袋で大切に包まれた「母子手帳」でした。JICA が紛争事情を抱えた国で作成を支援した、通称「生命（いのち）のパスポート」です。生後 10 ヵ月の赤ちゃんを連れたお母さんの持ち物だったそうです。子どもの安全と健康を願う心は、万国共有です。

Chapter 14

Review & Medical Reading

まとめと
医学英文読解

Chapter 8 から Chapter 13 で学んだ内容を復習しましょう。また、この章では、死亡率に関する英文を読んでみましょう。男女で部位別のがん死亡率にはどのような違いがあるでしょうか。

Q1 Put the words in order to form sentences.

1. I'll [you / bed / give / a / bath] now.
2. Please [your / towel / face / this / with / hot / wipe].
3. I'll [you / side / to / roll / one].
4. I'll [of / height / the bed / raise / the].
5. Would [to / hair / like / your / put / you] up?
6. I'll [hot / the / with / clean / basin / water / refill].

Q2 Read the description and find out what I am?

| nurse midwife | pharmacist | speech therapist | physical therapist |
| occupational therapist | clinical engineer | X-ray technician | medical clerk |

Description	My occupation
1. I help a person move his/her body again and improve their movement.	( )
2. I assist women in childbirth.	( )
3. I work in the nurses' station, answering phones, taking messages, and scheduling appointments.	( )
4. I help people with different speech and language disorders.	( )
5. I prepare and give your drugs and medicines.	( )
6. I am responsible for maintaining and operating the sophisticated medical equipment to treat patients.	( )

Q3 Complete the crossword below.

Across:

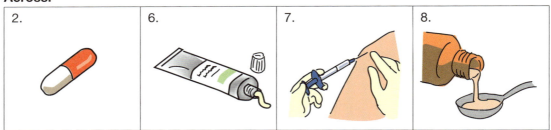

Down:

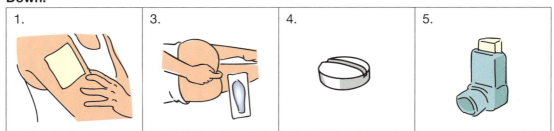

Chapter 14 Review & Medical Reading

Q4 Fill in the blanks with the given words.

| urinal | laxatives | urine | constipation | diarrhea | bedpan |

1. A person with loose bowels has (   ).

2. A person with difficulty in emptying the bowels has (   ).

3. (   ) are often used to relieve constipation.

4. Please collect a (   ) sample for a urinalysis.

5. A bedridden patient needs a (   ) to pass water in bed.

6. A bedridden patient needs a (   ) to have a bowel movement in bed.

Q5 Are these statements true (T) or false (F)?

1. (   ) Rapid triage is critical in cases of emergency.

2. (   ) The patient's heart stops beating, and he is not breathing at all, either. He needs CPA.

3. (   ) The pupil of the eye contracts in response to increased light. It is called a chief complaint.

4. (   ) My child is jerking and stiffening her arms and legs. She is having a seizure.

5. (   ) Your son is bleeding very badly. He needs CPR.

6. (   ) Your daughter is unconscious and does not respond to sounds. She is in a coma.

81

Q6 Match each chronic disease in English to the Japanese word:

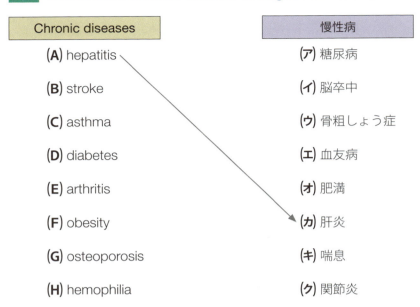

Q7 Fill in the blanks to match the Japanese sentences.

1. 最後の生理はいつでしたか。   When was your last (　　　　　)?
2. 初めての妊娠ですか。   Is this your first (　　　　　)?
3. 出産予定日はいつですか。   When is your (　　　　　) date?
4. 尿中のタンパクの値を調べます。   We'll test the (　　　　　) levels in your urine.
5. おしるしはありましたか。   Have you had any (　　　　　) yet?
6. 分娩室にお連れします。   I'll take you to the (　　　　　) room.

Chapter 14　Review & Medical Reading

Reading about Mortality Rates: 医学統計を読んでみましょう

ここでは、死因やがんの統計に関する医学統計を読んで、後の問いに答えましょう。

　71

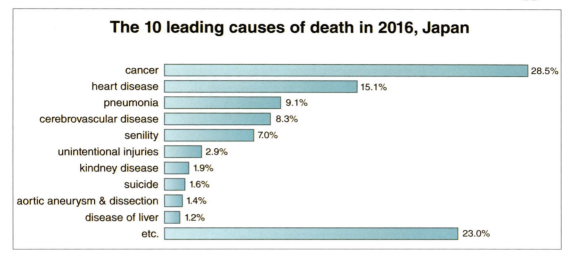

In 2016, cancer was the leading cause of death in Japan followed by heart diseases, pneumonia and cerebrovascular diseases. The number of cancer deaths has increased steadily and cancer became the top cause of death, surpassing cerebrovascular disease, in 1981.

Lung cancer became the major cause of cancer deaths among Japanese for the first time in 1998, surpassing stomach cancer, according to statistics compiled by the Ministry of Health, Labour and Welfare[5]. Lung and stomach cancers were followed by colon cancer, liver cancer and pancreatic cancer in men. The number of male cancer deaths was 1.5 times greater than that of female cancer deaths. And the risk of cancer is greater in older people.

The leading site for females was colon/rectum, followed by lung, stomach, pancreas, and breast. Breast cancer is the most common cause of death for women aged between 30 and 64 in Japan. Experts say that one in eleven people was suffering from the disease in 2016.

pneumonia＝肺炎
cerebrovascular＝脳血管の
surpassing＝〜を凌ぐ

statistics＝統計
compiled＝集められた
the Ministry of Health, Labour and Welfare＝厚生労働省

Q1 After reading the passage, fill in the blanks with the given diseases.

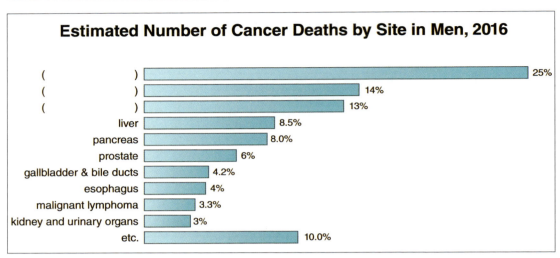

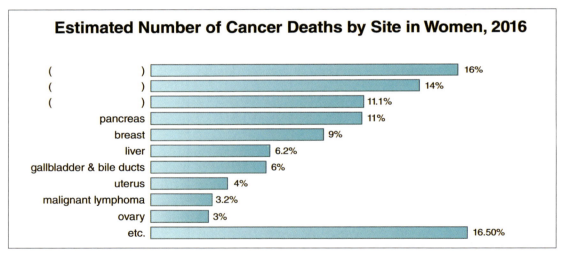

Q2 Are these statements true (T) or false (F)?

1. (　　) Lung cancer is the number 1 cause of death from disease in women in Japan.
2. (　　) Stomach cancer ranks second in cancer-killers among men in Japan.
3. (　　) The older you get, the more likely you are to get cancer.
4. (　　) One in eleven Japanese women suffers from colon/rectum cancer.
5. (　　) Cerebrovascular diseases were the leading cause of death until 1980 in Japan.
6. (　　) More women died of cancer than men in Japan.

References

(1) Peterson MC, et al. Contributions of the history, physical examination, and laboratory investigation in making medical diagnoses. West J Med.1992;156:163-165

(2) Yeaw J, et al. Comparing adherence and persistence across 6 chronic medication classes. J Manag Care Pharm. 2009;15(9):728-740

(3) Bobrow K, et al. Mobile Phone Text Messages to Support Treatment Adherence in Adults With High Blood Pressure (SMS-Text Adherence Support [StAR]): A Single-Blind, Randomized Trial. Circulation. 2016;133(6):592-600

(4) 独立行政法人国際協力機構 JICA
https://www.jica.go.jp/topics/2016/20160520_01.html

(5) 日本対がん協
https://www.jcancer.jp/en/cancer-in-japan

Web動画のご案内　StreamLine

本テキストの映像は、オンラインでのストリーミング再生になります。下記URLよりご利用ください。なお**有効期限は、はじめてログインした時点から1年半**です。

http://st.seibido.co.jp

①　ログイン画面

巻末に添付されているシールをはがして、アクセスコードをご入力ください。

②　メニュー画面

「Video」または「Audio」を選択すると、それぞれストリーミング再生ができます。

③　再生画面

推奨動作環境

【PC OS】
Windows 7〜 / Mac 10.8〜

【Mobile OS】
iOS / Android　※Androidの場合は4.x〜が推奨

【Desktop ブラウザ】
Internet Explorer 9〜 / Firefox / Chrome / Safari

TEXT PRODUCTION STAFF

edited by	編集
Takashi Kudo	工藤 隆志

cover design by	表紙デザイン
in-print	インプリント

text design by	本文デザイン
in-print	インプリント

cover illustration by	表紙イラスト
Kyoko Ogura	おぐら きょうこ

illustration by	イラスト
Yoko Sekine	関根 庸子

ANIMATION PRODUCTION STAFF

created by	制作
Minako Noda (fushigina)	野田 美波子（フシギナ）
Kenta Hiraku (fushigina)	比樂 健太（フシギナ）

music by	音楽
MusMus	ムズムズ

CD PRODUCTION STAFF

recorded by	吹き込み者
Carolyn Miller (AmE)	キャロリン・ミラー（アメリカ英語）
Jack Merluzzi (AmE)	ジャック・マルージ（アメリカ英語）
Rachel Walzer (AmE)	レイチェル・ワルザー（アメリカ英語）
Josh Keller (AmE)	ジョシュ・ケラー（アメリカ英語）
Karen Haedrich (AmE)	カレン・ヘドリック（アメリカ英語）

Talking with Your Patients in English
アニメで学ぶ看護英語

2019年1月20日　初版発行
2025年3月5日　第8刷発行

著　者　　平野 美津子
　　　　　Christine D. Kuramoto
　　　　　落合 亮太
発行者　　佐野 英一郎
発行所　　株式会社 成美堂
　　　　　〒101-0052　東京都千代田区神田小川町3-22
　　　　　TEL 03-3291-2261　FAX 03-3293-5490
　　　　　https://www.seibido.co.jp

印刷・製本　　倉敷印刷(株)

ISBN 978-4-7919-7193-0　　　　　　　　　　　　　Printed in Japan

・落丁・乱丁本はお取り替えします。
・本書の無断複写は、著作権上の例外を除き著作権侵害となります。

StreamLine **7193**

このシールをはがすと
StreamLineを視聴する
ためのアクセスコードが
記載されています。

定価2,750円（本体2,500円＋税10%）

ISBN978-4-7919-7193-0
C1082 ¥2500E

Talking with Your Patients in English

Chapter 1	Welcoming a Patient
Chapter 2	Taking Vital Signs
Chapter 3	Pain Assessment
Chapter 4	Feeling So Sick!
Chapter 5	Transferring a Patient
Chapter 6	Medical Departments
Chapter 7	Review & Medical Terminology
Chapter 8	Personal Care
Chapter 9	Giving Medication to a Patient
Chapter 10	Elimination (Bowel movement / Urination)
Chapter 11	Chronic Diseases
Chapter 12	Critical Care / Operating Room
Chapter 13	Pregnancy Check-up
Chapter 14	Review & Medical Reading

Medical Front Line

Kaoru Masago　　Hiroaki Tanaka　　Bill Benfield